On the Meaning of Sex

J. Budziszewski

Wilmington, Delaware

Library of Congress Cataloging-in-Publication Data

Budziszewski, J., 1952–
 On the meaning of sex / J. Budziszewski.
 p. cm.
 Includes bibliographical references and index.
 ISBN 978-1-935191-24-7

1. Sex. I. Title.

HQ21.B8784 2011
306.7—dc23

 2011033481

Published in the United States by:

ISI Books
Intercollegiate Studies Institute
3901 Centerville Road
Wilmington, Delaware 19807-1938
www.isibooks.org

Manufactured in the United States of America

Second printing, January 2013

There He taught me the science full of sweetness.
—John of the Cross

To Sandra

Contents

1

Does Sex Have to Mean Something?

Where have You hidden Yourself,
And abandoned me in my groaning, O my Beloved?
You have fled like the hart,
Having wounded me.
I ran after You, crying; but You were gone.
                    —John of the Cross, *Spiritual Canticle*

One day in class, there loomed up into the discussion of old books the barren playland of Aldous Huxley's *Brave New World*, that posthuman wilderness where it is the "duty" of people to be infantile, even if they wish not to be—a wish that conditioning makes impossible for all but a few. Most of the students had read the book, and remembered passages like the following:

> "It suddenly struck me the other day," continued Bernard, "that it might be possible to be an adult all the time."
> "I don't understand." Lenina's tone was firm.

"I know you don't. And that's why we went to bed together yesterday—like infants—instead of being adults and waiting."

"But it was fun," Lenina insisted. "Wasn't it?"

"Oh, the greatest fun," he answered, but in a voice so mournful, with an expression so profoundly miserable, that Lenina felt all her triumph suddenly evaporate. Perhaps he had found her too plump, after all.[1]

Though not by precisely the same methods as in Huxley's world, students these days are pretty thoroughly conditioned, so most were on Lenina's side. Why anyone should feel anything amiss in such a world was a mystery to them. If everyone is having fun, then what could be the problem?

But Harris, in the first row, disagreed. In fact, he was revolted. "Those people are disgusting," he said.

Thinking that I got his point, I gave a premature nod. "Sex ought to mean something," I remarked.

"No," he replied, to my surprise. "Sex *doesn't* always have to mean something."

That threw me a little off balance, and before I could shake myself out of teacher-trance, someone else spoke up, turning the discussion in another direction, and the moment was lost.

After class ended, when students were filing from the room, I asked Harris to wait a moment. "Your comment about Huxley's people—obviously I misunderstood what you were getting at. But if sex doesn't have to mean anything, then why did they revolt you?"

"The way they make babies—in factories, without parents," he replied. "The whole thing about 'decanting' them from glass bottles. *That's* what's disgusting." Unfortunately, we both had someplace else to go, and as though we were acting out a parable of Huxleyan disconnection, for a second time the contact was broken.

That was a failure of teaching. I've tried to make up for it since then, and this book is part of the attempt.

One might ask: So what if the contact failed? Did that matter? After all, the puzzle had been cleared up anyway, hadn't it? I asked Harris what he had meant, and Harris told me. Babies shouldn't be industrially produced, check. But sex itself doesn't have to mean anything, check. We might disagree about the second point, but at least we both knew what he'd been getting at.

But did we both know? I don't think we did. What issue had our brief exchange of comments really presented?

At first I thought that the issue was merely whether sex has to mean something. My answer to the question was "Yes," Harris's "No."

But the real question wasn't that at all. It was how sex can both mean something, and also not mean anything. To be even more precise, it was how sex can both *always* mean something, and also *never* mean anything. I draw this conclusion because Harris's opinion was at variance with his emotion.

He said sex doesn't have to mean anything. If it doesn't "have to" mean anything, that means it doesn't ever mean anything really—at least it doesn't ever mean anything in any way that could restrict our choices. Behind sex is nothing but a void. And yet, for some reason, Harris was revolted by the factory production of children in canisters. The void was not empty after all. For if it was really a void, then how could he be revolted? How could one be disgusted by nothing?

I hear the objection already. You're getting worked up over nothing, Professor. Feelings don't make sense. Is that so? I give people more credit than that. Every feeling makes some kind of sense, even if only confusedly. So I ask again: Why was Harris revolted?

Presumably, what bothered him about the assembly-line production of babies was that it sliced the conjugal union of the mother and the father out of the picture. But if sex doesn't have to mean anything, then so what if that was sliced out? It shouldn't have bothered Harris unless procreation is something that ought to take place in the loving embrace of the parents. But if so, then in the depths of his mind, didn't he recognize that sex means something after all? In fact, didn't he recognize that it means at least two connected things—an aspiration to children, and an aspiration to union?—the act by which babies are made, and the act by which their parents are united? Moreover, since Harris was revolted that the aspiration to children could ever be separated from the aspiration to union, it would seem that he recognized that these two meanings aren't merely sometimes joined together, but that they are joined whenever we have sex. In short, although he reported that sex doesn't always have to mean anything, his loathing for factory production of children told the story that it means something already, and it means it all the time.

The fact that he asserted the opposite opinion doesn't wipe out our conclusion. It only makes it more mysterious. Apparently sex means something to us even if we don't admit to ourselves that it does.

Let us look a little more closely into this mystery. What did Harris think he meant—what was he trying to get at—when he said that sex doesn't always have to mean something? One of the reasons I am interested in the answer to that question is that it seems to me that a lot of people are trying to get at the same thing.

One might be tempted to think that he wasn't getting

at anything in particular, that he was just confused. No doubt he was confused, but airy dismissals of this sort don't treat people with the respect that their confusion deserves. It is childish to dismiss someone's thoughts as unworthy of consideration just because they are mixed up; human beings are always trying to get at something, even when they don't know what it is. The oft-derided truth that man is a rational being does not mean that he always thinks clearly. But he always thinks something, so what, in this case, was that something?

If I had questioned Harris further—"What do you mean when you say sex doesn't have to mean anything? Do people engage in it for no reason at all? Does it just happen, like a gurgle in the stomach, a can rattling down the street, or a screen door blowing shut in the breeze?"—perhaps he would have conceded that sex does have trivial meanings: a little pleasure, a little fun, a little relief from boredom and desire. This wouldn't be much of a concession. Sex would mean something, but only in the way that eating a peanut means something, chewing on an ice cube means something, scratching an itch means something. There would be no more call to rhapsodize about the touch of a man and a woman than to compose sonnets about the communion of a picnicker with his mayonnaise. Maybe less.

But a response like that would not get us any further in reconciling what Harris said with what his emotion implied. So let us start at the other end. Let us start, not with his opinion, but with his revulsion.

When Harris described his aversion toward the factory production of children, he seemed to be saying that it is wrong to separate procreation from the act of union. On the other hand, when he said that sex doesn't have to mean anything, he seemed to be saying that it *is* all right to separate the act of union from procreation. That is like saying that you may take the seeds from the apple, but you may not take the apple from the seeds. This, of course, is nonsense. To sever A from B is to sever B from A.

Perhaps what Harris was getting at—I don't mean what he was thinking, but what he might have meant to think, what he might have started to think if I had pressed him—was a bit different. Perhaps the idea is that it is all right to separate *our* meaning for sex from *the* meaning for sex—to separate what sex means for us from what, simply, it means. Just because something disgusts us, he might say, that doesn't mean we shouldn't do it.

If I could make Harris speak like a philosopher, perhaps he would concede that from the perspective of human nature, the two meanings of sex are joined like the apple with the seeds, but perhaps he would also insist that we aren't slaves to nature. After all, don't we breed such things as seedless apples? Perhaps he would say that human will is greater than human nature. Perhaps he would say that from this different and higher perspective, the perspective of the will, the meanings of sex are merely options, like items on the shelf of a pantry. Nothing prevents someone from removing the sack of sugar but leaving the flour behind, or for that matter leaving both behind and opening the refrigerator instead. Perhaps Harris would say that making choices in just that way—"thus I will it, and so thus it is"—is what it means to be free.

I realize that in making Harris speak like a philosopher I am asking a lot from my readers. There are limits to the suspension of disbelief. We all know that undergraduates don't speak like that. True, but they think like that. Someone might protest, "No, they don't even think like that." This is only half true. They don't think like that clearly, but they think like that vaguely. I suspect that the words I've put in Harris's mouth are pretty close to what he was vaguely trying to say, and I more than suspect that a great many other people are vaguely trying to say the same thing. So allow the words I have put in his mouth to remain there.

Even so, they leave us with a problem. In fact they leave us with three problems.

The first of these problems is that meaning isn't arbitrary. Yes, we can associate sex in our minds with anything we choose—with pain, pleasure, tedium, amusement, alienation, reconciliation, fertility, sterility, misery, joy, life, death, or what have you. This is true of all things, not just sex. We can associate anything with anything; as Katherine Hepburn's character declared in the romantic comedy *Desk Set*, "I associate many things with many things." I may associate friendship with betrayal because my friend was untrue. I may associate birth with death because my child was stillborn. I may associate emptiness with intelligence because I have read too much Sartre. Even so, the meaning of friendship as such is not betrayal, the meaning of birth as such is not death, and the meaning of emptiness as such is not intelligence. If anything whatsoever could mean anything whatsoever—if girls in straw hats could mean jars of processed cheese, or children on swings could mean termites in the walls—then nothing could mean anything in particular. Language itself would be pointless. We might as well give it up and just bubble our lips. Even the statement that sex doesn't have to mean anything is intelligible only against the background of a world in which, in general, things do mean something.

And if other things do mean something, then why shouldn't sex mean something? Why should something as powerful and interesting as sex be the exception?

The second problem is that human nature is not a master, distinct from us, reducing us to bondage. It is the deep structure of what we really are. The fact that we are not free to be other than human doesn't mean that we aren't free; how could it truly be freedom to be false to ourselves? Blue may as well demand the liberty to be red, odd the liberty to be even, vegetable the liberty to be mineral. That kind of liberty is just the liberty of self-annihilation. But if true freedom doesn't lie in being false to ourselves, then as the old adage claims, it must lie in being true to ourselves. Either this ancient recommendation is fatuous—for we are already ourselves, and cannot help but be ourselves, in the mere sense that we do what our wills bid us do—or it means directing our wills in such a way that the meanings and purposes that lie fallow in our nature can unfold. By the latter test, everything is free only when its nature is unfolding. An acorn is free only when it is coming to be an oak.

But if we are free only when our nature is unfolding, then shouldn't this be true of our sexual nature, too? Shouldn't we direct our wills in such a way that the meanings and purposes that lie fallow in sexuality can unfold?

The third problem is that human will isn't something separate from human nature, but a part of human nature. At best, when someone says that his will is greater than his nature, he is badly expressing the idea that his will is greater than the *rest* of his nature—that his nature does matter, and that his will is its best and noblest part—that it acquires from this nobility a royal right to rule all the rest of the kingdom. So perhaps we come even closer to the latent intention of Harris's words if we say that freedom is not freedom from the reign of human nature, but freedom of the highest part of human nature to exercise dominion over its lower parts. So far as it goes, I think that principle is true.

But is the highest part of our nature really the will? Isn't the highest part rather the intelligence that directs the will? Wouldn't one of the highest functions of this intelligence be *recognizing* the meanings embedded in the lovely array of the rest of the parts of our nature? In fact, hadn't Harris's moment of revulsion brought him to the very edge of recognizing some of these meanings? I think that it had, though I am pretty sure that he wasn't paying attention.

There are more mysteries here, such as why, if it is impossible to transcend our nature, we imagine that we would like to. We cannot literally be other than what we are. Yet is there some other sense in which we might transcend ourselves? Is it possible that the confused desire for self-transcendence might really, unknown to Harris, be an even stronger motive in his heart of hearts than a little pleasure, a little fun, a little relief from boredom and desire? Might it even be possible that these little motives of pleasure and distraction are only masks for the greater motive, that they are cases of mistaken identification? Could this be one of the reasons *why* we are so confused about what we are getting at, contradicting ourselves at every step, feeling so strongly about things that a moment before we insisted didn't matter?

I am trying to say too much at once. First things first. So many more elementary things have to be considered in this book before we can return to such questions as the ones I have raised. For now, let me call an end to my imaginary interrogation of poor Harris. He is paying a pretty high price for my failure to teach him that day.

Ah, but perhaps it is already too late. Even if I do finally call an end to the interrogation of Harris, I have already read far too much into his offhand remarks. In one sense: Yes, of course I have. Surely he wasn't consciously thinking all those thoughts I attributed to him. But in another sense: No, of course I haven't. All these thoughts were hovering around him like ghosts, like leaves drifting dimly through a pond.

Why such an effort to gather those drifting leaves? I offer the following defense.

In the first place, I owe it to Harris. However a teacher may fall short, that is his calling. In the second place, when I speculate that Harris might say this, or might say that, I am not relying simply on my actual knowledge of Harris, which is slim. I am supplementing my reflections about Harris's state of mind with the ruminated-upon memories of my own conversations throughout life, dialogues with others, colloquies with myself. Finally, allow me to point out that human beings know a great deal more than they are usually aware of knowing, and Harris was no exception. So much of our knowledge is latent, "in potentiality," not yet fully actualized.

When latent knowledge does break the surface, the experience is more like remembering something than like thinking of something. Ordinary language has an armory of expressions for this. We say things like "I didn't know I knew that," "I thought it must be something like that," or "I never thought of that, but somehow I knew it all along."

It is too late for me to evoke that sort of response from Harris, but I would consider the book successful if even just now and then, it evoked that sort of response from a few of its readers.

Why write a book on this topic at all? Various motives commingle. A great one is gratitude, because the experience of love is the great redeeming experience of my life. I am referring to all sorts of loves, the love of parents, teachers, friends. But I am especially referring to the love of my wife, which reawakened me when I was lost in a solipsistic maze and had lost what Dante calls "the intelligence of love." The meaning of the intercession of Beatrice, in

Dante's trip through the nether regions, has never been mysterious to me, for through this love there also came the fragrance of the love of God.

There, I have uttered it, the forbidden word: "God." That will be quite enough to make some people dismiss this book as "religious," and therefore irrelevant to their concerns. How can I reassure them? In one way, I can't. If divine grace is real, then it is as inescapably relevant to human life as oxygen to breathing. In another way, I can. I promise not to touch on the forbidden subject again until—

Hold, that is too much! Before I finalize the promise, let me qualify it. I promise not to wade into a full-blown discussion of grace until the end, but I do not vow not to allude to it. Those who wish to be spared the repetition of my opening offense, the mention of God just above, may pass over such light mentions. If it would make them more comfortable, they might pretend that my allusions to God are merely phatic utterances, like "How do you do?" When they do get to the distasteful final chapter, they may skip it. In the meantime, such as it is, the argument will sustain itself by reference to human realities that anyone might be able to know, whether he is "religious" or not.

But I was speaking of my motives. Another motive for writing this book is the desire for a certain kind of beauty, the beauty of understanding. I want to possess the beauty of the wisdom of love. I want to net that magical bird. No one seems to know where she lives. The hunter sets out on his pursuit from a world so uninterested in finding her that shops sell Valentine's Day greeting cards featuring photographs of buttocks with coarse sayings sprayed across them in red paint. Someone might say that no one should write a book until he is in full possession of the quarry he seeks, but in that case no one should write a book, because in this life knowledge comes little by little. I don't say I have netted my beautiful bird and compelled her to tell me all, but no one can ardently pursue her without catching a few glimpses and passing sparkles of her loveliness. Otherwise, who would have the heart to continue the hunt? Whoever has a little lore must share it with his fellow hunters.

The final motive for writing such a book is that my eyes are so full of the pain I see around me that if I did not have the relief of writing, they would be full of tears instead. Errors about sex cause such terrible suffering, in our day more than in most. The worst is the suffering of those who no longer know they are in torment, for it is simply a lie that everyone is happy who believes himself happy, a slander that nobody is suffering unless he thinks that he is. I would wish these sufferers joy, but if by writing the book I could do no more than dip the end of my finger in water to cool their tongues, then that would be wish enough.

For whom have I written? For my own generation; for the generation just coming into its power; and for the generation just coming over the horizon. For my own generation, which invented the sexual revolution, the train may seem to have left the station. We treated our friends, our spouses, and our children dreadfully, especially our children. That hurt is irrevocably done. It is too late to repair everything, but it is not too late to repair something, and it is never too late to repent. (Is that another religious reference, a breach of authorial promise? But surely an atheist could be sorry for something, even if he didn't know to whom he should be sorry.) To return to the thread, there is a partnership among the generations, however we may dishonor that partnership. Perhaps we can do better with our children's children than most of us did with our own.

For the generation coming into its power, I would wish the ability not to compound the mistakes that mine has made, and perhaps even the ability to discern some of those mistakes for what they are. One might think the second wish is easy. To recognize the mistakes of the previous generation, one only needs to keep one's eyes open. In a sense, yes. The light is certainly bright enough. The problem is that it is almost too bright; it is hard to keep one's eyes open in the glare. One suffers an overwhelming temptation to look away from those scorching desert scenes and gaze at mirages instead. There is even a certain tendency to punish those who do try to see. A case in point: At the dawn of the sexual revolution, social scientists produced statistical studies purporting to show that children are better off when quarreling parents divorce, that broken homes are just as functional as intact ones, and that cohabitation has no influence on the stability of a subsequent marriage. As anyone conversant with the field now knows, newer and more careful studies show all that to be wildly false. A young, untenured family sociologist whom I know used to circulate the results of these new studies secretly among other scholars. But he asked me and his other friends never to mention his name. Why? Because calling the mirage a mirage is a good way to end a career.

For the generation coming over the horizon, I wish ease from their burdens, for unfortunately, the errors of my generation and the one after it have already been compounded. I used to lead my students through an exercise that parallels the argument of Aristotle's classic work, the *Nicomachean Ethics*. Like him, I asked, "What is happiness?" Like his, my students used to give answers like "pleasure," "friendship," and "success." Like him, I encouraged them to scrutinize each of these common answers more deeply. In recent years, however, the exercise has started to fail. The last time I asked my students, "What is happiness?" the first half-dozen all gave variations on the answer, "freedom from pain and suffering." The negative element so filled their eyes that they were completely unable to suggest anything positive that happiness might mean.

My guess is that my students have lived all their young lives in pursuit of pleasure—as the young generally do—but with less restraint from our crumbling conventions than the young have lived their lives in previous generations. Consequently, even at this tender age, they have begun to experience the hedonistic paradox, which usually kicks in much later. He who makes pleasure the object of his life eventually finds that it evaporates; he who fails to distinguish between good and bad pleasures ends in misery. Although my students don't formulate the paradox explicitly, they feel it in their bones.

On the far side of the paradox lies the insight that pleasure comes as a by-product of pursuing what is good in itself. Alas, few of my students get to the far side. Their parents, friends, and teachers, led on by the mighty enchanters of culture, blare in their ears that pleasure simply is the good in itself. Consequently, their first cheerful idea, that happiness is pleasure, suffers a dark transmutation into the equally naïve, but morbid idea, that happiness is just absence of pain. And that is what they say in my classroom. Not many of them look happy. Each year they have less sense of humor. They show all the signs of exhaustion. Though they have never heard of Schopenhauer, they are intuitive Schopenhauerians. Although they may say things like "I am having an awesome life!"—as one of them did—they grow weary in the midst of excitements.

Still thinking of the same generation, a related reason for writing the book is that it is dangerous to say much about these things in the classroom, and safer to say them in a book—which, on a lark, a few refugees from the classroom may even read. Writing a book is risky too, but the medium of print is somewhat cooler. Of course, sometimes when I speak about these things in the classroom, nothing happens. But sometimes something does. Some students may cry. Others may rage. A few like to bait their professor, which I wouldn't mind if it were just a game—teachers need a sense of humor, too. But campuses have speech codes these days, whether admitted or not, and one does not relish the prospect of being brought up on charges before the thought police. If you think there could be no danger in answering a simple question from a student, think again!

Since I knew what I wanted to say in this book, since its argument is not particularly dense, and since I have some experience putting words together, the book should have been easy to write. Two things have made it surprisingly difficult. The first is that it is harder to write about what is obvious but unrecognized than about what is really obscure. The second is that when everything is topsy-turvy and confused, it is hard to know where to begin.

One of the two friends and editors who urged me to write the book suggested that I take the article that is now chapter two and "just add water."[2] He didn't mean that I should dilute it. What he really meant, to change the metaphor, was that I should remove its screws and fasteners, break it apart into sections, and puff up each section into a separate chapter. Unfortunately, the self-contained design of chapter two does not lend itself to this procedure, and besides, the chapter's topic was only one of many topics that I wanted to explore.

For this reason, I have followed a different path. I have taken inventory of the biggest of those topsy-turvy things, those things the topsy-turviness of which make the path to the beauty I was speaking of most difficult to follow. To each, one chapter is devoted. The result is not complete. But I have not aspired to completeness. Sometimes, less is more.

One more thing. This book is about the meaning of the human realities related to sex, not about the bitter objections some make to these meanings. Some years ago, during the question and answer period following an invited public lecture I gave someplace or other, the young man who headed one of the local student activist groups stood and haughtily took me to task for what I had said in my talk about Hot Button Issue Q. The amusing thing about the incident is that I had uttered scarcely a word in my talk about Q. I had merely devoted a sentence to the meaning of an obscure statement that someone else had once made about Q. No matter. For him, it seemed, the reasons for coming to a lecture had nothing to do with listening to what the speaker had to say. They were all about what he wanted to say, which was all about his anger and self-importance.

There is a time to speak of the things that the young man harangued me about, but for the purposes of this book, they would merely be distractions. If anyone wants to work out the further implications of the premises that I develop here only in part, he is free to do so, but he will be on his own.

Looking out over the sexual landscape of our time I see a terrain of unutterable sweetness, despoiled by unmentionable pain. Yet who knows? Perhaps it is not too late to redeem the unutterable sweetness. Shall we try to find out?

2

The Meaning of the Sexual Powers

There you will show me
That which my soul desired;
And there You will give at once,
O You, my life!
That which You gave me the other day.
                    —John of the Cross, *Spiritual Canticle*

Midnight. Shelly is getting herself drunk so that she can bring herself to go home with the strange man seated next to her at the bar. **One o'clock.** Steven is busy downloading pornographic images of children from internet bulletin boards. **Two o'clock.** Marjorie, who used to spend every Friday night in bed with a different man, has been bingeing and purging since eleven. **Three o'clock.** Pablo stares through the darkness at his ceiling, wondering how to convince his girlfriend to have an abortion. **Four o'clock.** After partying all night, Jesse takes another man home, not mentioning that he tests positive for an incurable STD. **Five o'clock.** Lisa is in the bathroom, cutting herself delicately but compulsively with a razor. She isn't trying to kill herself. She doesn't understand why she does it. She does it often.

This isn't what my generation expected when it invented the sexual revolution. The game isn't fun anymore. Even some of the diehard proponents of that enslaving liberation have begun to show signs of fatigue and confusion. Naomi Wolf, in her book *Promiscuities*, reports that when she lost her own virginity at age fifteen, there was "something important missing."[1] Apparently, the thing missing was the very sense that anything could be important. In her book *Last Night in Paradise*, Katie Roiphe poignantly wonders what could be wrong with freedom: "It's not the absence of rules exactly, the dizzying sense that we can do whatever we want, but the sudden realization that nothing we do matters."[2] Desperate to find a way to make it matter, some young male homosexuals court death, deliberately seeking out men with deadly infections as partners; this is called "bug chasing."[3] At the opposite extreme, some of those who languish in the shadow of the revolution toy with the idea of abstinence—but an abstinence that arises less from purity or principle than from boredom, fear, and disgust. In Hollywood, of all places, it has become fashionable to talk up Buddhism, a doctrine which finds the cure for suffering in the ending of desire, and the cure for desire in annihilation.

Speaking of exhaustion, let me tell you about my students. In the '80s, if I suggested in class that there might be any problem with sexual liberation, they said that everything was fine—what was I talking about? Now if I raise questions, many of them speak differently. They still live like libertines, sometimes they still talk like libertines, but it's getting old. They are beginning to sound like the children of third-generation Maoists. My generation may have ordered the sexual revolution, but theirs is paying the price.

I am not speaking only of the medical price. To be sure, that price is ruinous: At the beginning of the revolution, most physicians had to worry about only two or three sexually transmitted diseases, and now it is more like two or three dozen. But I am not speaking only of broken bodies. Consider, for example, broken childhoods. What is it like for your family to break up because dad has found someone new, then to break up again because mom has? What is it like to be passed from stepparent to stepparent to stepparent? What is it like to grow up knowing that you would have had a sister, but she was aborted?

A young man remarked in one of my classes that he longed to get married and stay married to the same woman forever, but because his own parents hadn't been able to manage it, he was afraid to get married at all. Women show signs of avoidance too, but in a more conflicted way. According to a survey commissioned by the Independent Women's Forum, 83 percent of college women say marriage is a very important goal for them. Yet 40 percent of them engage in "hooking up"—physical encounters (commonly oral sex) without any expectation of relationship whatsoever.[4] Do you hear a little cognitive dissonance there? Can you think of a sexual behavior less likely to get you into marriage? The ideology of hooking up says that sex is merely release or recreation. You have some friends for friendship and you have other friends just for hooking up—they're called "friends with benefits." What your body does is unrelated to your heart. Don't believe it. The same survey reports that hooking up commonly takes place when both participants are drinking or drunk, and it's not hard to guess the reason why: After a certain amount of this, you may need to get drunk to go through with it.

The fact is that we aren't designed for hooking up. Our hearts and bodies are designed to work together. Truly, don't we already know that? A writer who interviewed teenagers who hook up supplies a telling anecdote. The girl Melissa tells him, "I have my friends for my emotional needs, so I don't need that from the guy I'm having sex with." Yet on the day of the interview, "Melissa was in a foul mood. Her 'friend with benefits' had just broken up with her. 'How is that even possible?' she said, sitting, shoulders slumped, in a booth at a diner. 'The point of having a friend with benefits is that you won't get broken up with, you won't get hurt.'" [5]

But let there be no mistake: When I say we aren't designed for this sort of thing, I'm not just speaking for females. A woman may be more likely to cry the next morning; it's not so easy to sleep with a man who won't even call you back. But a man pays a price, too. He probably thinks he can instrumentalize his relationships with women in general, yet remain capable of romantic intimacy when the right woman comes along. Sorry, fellow. That's not how it works. Sex is like applying adhesive tape; promiscuity is like ripping the tape off again. If you rip it off, rip it off, rip it off, eventually the tape can't stick anymore.

The ruin of the adhesive probably contributes to an even wider social problem that might be called the Peter Pan syndrome. Men in their forties with children in their twenties talk like boys in their teens. "I still don't feel like a grown-up," they say. They don't even call themselves men—just "guys."

Now in a roundabout sort of way, I've just introduced the concept of natural law. Although the natural law tradition is unfamiliar to most people today, it has been the main axis of Western ethical thought for twenty-three centuries, and in fact it is experiencing a modest renaissance. The hinge concept is meaning and design. I said that we're not designed for hooking up, that we're designed for our bodies and hearts to work together. We human beings really do have a design, and I mean that term in the broadest sense: not merely mechanical design (this part goes here, this part goes there), but what kind of being we are. Because the design is not merely biological, but also emotional, intellectual, and spiritual, the languages of natural law, natural design, natural meanings, and natural purposes are intertranslatable, and most of the time interchangeable. Some ways of living comport with our design. Others don't.

From a natural law perspective, the problem with twenty-first-century Western sexuality is that it flouts the embedded principles and the inbuilt meanings of the human sexual design. A medical scientist or practitioner might highlight the consequences of flouting the biological side of the design, focusing on unexpected pregnancies or sexually transmitted diseases. A natural law philosopher like me will probably highlight the consequences of flouting the other side of the design, speaking about women who wake up crying and men who are afraid to grow up or get married. But these two sides of human sexuality are interwoven, and must be viewed as they are.

Then what are the meanings and purposes embedded in the human sexual design, and how do they harmonize? What are the sexual powers for? What are they about? I'll answer this question in a moment. Before I can do so, I have to take time out to deal with three inevitable objections.

The first objection is that it is rubbish to talk about natural meanings and purposes, because we merely imagine such things. According to the objector's way of thinking, meanings and purposes aren't natural—they aren't really in the things themselves—they are merely in the eye of the beholder. But is this true? Take the lungs, for example. When we say that their purpose is to oxygenate the blood, are we just making that up? Of course not. The purpose of oxygenation isn't in the eye of the beholder; it's in the design of the lungs themselves. There is no reason for us to have lungs apart from it. Suppose a young man is more interested in using his lungs to get high by sniffing glue. What would you think of me if I said, "That's interesting—I guess the purpose of *my* lungs is to oxygenate my blood, but the purpose of his lungs is to get high?" You'd think me a fool, and rightly so. By sniffing glue, he doesn't change the purpose built into his lungs, he only violates it. We can ascertain the purposes of the other features of our design in the same way. The purpose of the eyes is to see, the purpose of the heart is to pump blood, the purpose of the thumb is to oppose the fingers so as to grasp, the purpose of the capacity for anger is to protect endangered goods, and so on. If we can ascertain the meanings and purposes of all those other powers, there is no reason to think that we cannot ascertain the meanings and purposes of the sexual powers. Natural function and personal meaning are not alien to each other. They are connected. In a rightly ordered way of thinking, they turn out to be different angles of vision on the same thing.

The second objection is that it doesn't make any difference even if we can ascertain the meanings or purposes of the sexual powers, because an *is* does not imply an *ought*. This dogma too is false. If the purpose of eyes is to see, then eyes that see well are good eyes, and eyes that see poorly are poor ones. Given their purpose, this is what it *means* for eyes to be good. Moreover, good is to be pursued; the appropriateness of pursuing it is what it means for anything to be good. Therefore, the appropriate thing to do with poor eyes is try to turn them into good ones. If it really were impossible to derive an *ought* from the *is* of the human design, then the practice of medicine would make no sense. Neither would the practice of health education. Consider the young glue-sniffer again. How should we advise him? Is the purpose of his lungs irrelevant? Should we say to him, "Sniff all you want, because an *is* does not imply an *ought*"? Of course not; we should advise him to kick the habit. We ought to respect the *is* of our design. Nothing in us should be put into action in a way that flouts its inbuilt meanings and purposes.

The third objection is that I am not really speaking of natural purposes, but only of natural functions—that I am attributing mind-like qualities to things. But I am doing no such thing. The term "purpose" is used to signify that something is ordered or directed to an end. Such order is present in one way in things, in another way in our minds, and in still another way in the mind of God. If it offends you to think of the third way, then for purposes of this chapter, just think of the first and the second. Now the mode in which purpose is present in things is different from the mode in which it is present in minds, for a thing has no understanding of the matter, but a mind does. The term "function" merely signifies the mode in which purpose is present in things rather than in minds. No sane person imagines that eyes know that their purpose is to see. Yet seeing is truly their purpose; that is what they are for. That suffices for the reply to the objection, but I am not finished; there is one more thing to be said. The purposes in our bodies and the purposes in our minds must harmonize, because we are composite beings. We are not mind alone or flesh alone, but mind and flesh united, incarnate mind and personalized flesh. What sense would it make for my mind and my body to be at war? Should I pluck out my eyes, crying, "seeing is not my purpose, seeing is just a function, it has nothing to do with the true me?"

No, because my eyes are part of the true me, part of my body and soul unity. So it is with all the other things in our nature, not just our eyes and hearts but our sexual powers.

What then are the natural meanings and purposes of the sexual powers? One is procreation—the bringing about and nurture of new life, the formation of families in which children have moms and dads. The other is union—the mutual and total self-giving and accepting of two polar, complementary selves in their entirety, soul and body. These two meanings are so tightly stitched that we can start with either one and follow the threads to the other.

But why *these* purposes? Why not say that the meaning and purpose of the sexual powers is pleasure? Certainly sex is pleasurable, but there is nothing distinctive about that. In various ways and degrees, the exercise of every voluntary power is pleasurable. It is pleasurable to eat, pleasurable to breath, even pleasurable to flex the muscles of the leg. The problem is that eating is pleasurable even if I am eating too much, breathing is pleasurable even if I am sniffing glue, flexing the muscles of the leg is pleasurable even if I am kicking the dog. For a criterion of when it is good to enjoy each pleasure, one must look beyond the fact that it is a pleasure. Consider an analogy between sex and eating. The purpose of eating is to take in nutrition, but eating is pleasurable, so suppose that we were to say that the purpose of eating is pleasure, too. Then it would seem that any way of eating that gives pleasure is good, whether it is suitable for nutrition or not. Certain ancient Romans are said to have thought this way. To prolong the pleasure of their feasts, they purged between courses. I hope it is not difficult to recognize that such behavior is disordered.

The more general point I am trying to make is that although we find pleasure in exercising our sexual powers, pleasure is not their purpose; it only provides a motive for using these powers, and a dangerous one, too, which may at times conflict with their true purposes and steer us wrong. Besides, to think of pleasure as the purpose of intercourse is to treat our bodies merely as tools for sending agreeable sensations to our minds. They are of inestimably greater dignity than that, for they are part of what we are.

Let us begin, then, with procreation. Two conditions must be satisfied before one can say that the purpose of anything (call it P) is to bring about something else (call it Q), and procreation satisfies both of them.[6] First, it must be the case that P actually does bring about Q, and the sexual powers do bring about procreation. Second, the causal connection of P with Q must be part of the explanation of why we have P in the first place. Procreation satisfies this condition, too; apart from the link between the sexual powers and new life, any explanation of why we have sexual powers at all would be woefully incomplete. I think even the most ardent Darwinist would concede this point. (By the way, if you have been worrying about a population explosion, you can stop. In the developed countries, the net reproduction rate is 0.7 and dropping, which means that the next generation will be only 70 percent as large as this one. Demographers are beginning to realize that the looming threat throughout most of the world is not explosion, but implosion.)[7]

If the procreative meaning of sex is granted, the unitive meaning follows. We aren't designed like guppies, who cooperate only for a moment. For us, procreation requires an enduring partnership between two beings the man and the woman, who are different, but in ways that enable them to complete and balance each other. Union, then, characterizes the distinctly human mode of procreation. A parent of each sex is necessary to make the child, to raise the child, and to teach the child. Both are needed to make him, because the female provides the egg, the male fertilizes it, and the female incubates the resulting zygote. Both are needed to raise him, because the male is better suited to protection, the female to nurture. Both are needed to teach him, because he needs a model of his own sex, a model of the other, and a model of the relationship between them. Mom and dad are jointly irreplaceable. Their partnership in procreation continues even after the kids are grown, because the kids need the help and counsel of their parents to establish their own new families.

Sociologists Sara S. McLanahan and Gary Sandefur remark that "If we were asked to design a system for making sure that children's basic needs were met, we would probably come up with something quite similar to the two-parent ideal."[8] Of course, for it is designed, though not by us. René König, another sociologist, explains that children, young ones especially, thrive less in orphanages than in the average family—even when care is taken to make the institutions homelike, and even when, to sociological eyes, they are better organized than an average family in every way that can be measured: hygienically, medically, psychologically, and pedagogically.[9] Plainly, the union of the spouses is at the center of our procreative design. Without it, procreative partnerships could hardly be expected to endure in such a way as to generate sound and stable families.

How astonishing it is, this business of the mutual donation of selves. New human life could have been brought about asexually, as in yeast and amoebas. It might have been brought about sexually but non-unitively, as in those guppies I mentioned. It might even have been brought about by some sort of lifelong pairing without the gift of self, as in certain birds. But it isn't; for us, sex is something different. Besides the potentiality for procreation—*because* of its potentiality for procreation—it also carries within it the potentiality for a powerful and distinct form of human love. This is why sex shakes us to the core, this is why it says, "Now you will never be the same."

The unitive meaning of sex is so important that the argument works just as well in the opposite direction. What I mean is that instead of starting with the procreative purpose and then considering how it is connected with union, we can start with the unitive meaning of sex and then consider how it is connected with procreation. Why is this so? Because the meaning of union is inseparably bonded to the powers which bring union about. We join ourselves by doing what? By an act which is intrinsically open to the possibility of new life. In other words, whenever I give myself sexually, I am doing something that *cannot help but mean* that happy chance. Someone might object, "That's not true. The chance of new life isn't a meaning of sex, at least not for me, because I don't want it. I even take steps to prevent it." I'm sorry, but what you intend subjectively can't change what your act means objectively. A bodily action is like a word; we mean things to each other no less by what we do than by what we say. In fact, when the speech of the mouth contradicts the speech of the body, the body's speech repeals the mouth's. To crush your windpipe with my thumbs is to say to you, "Now die," even if I tell you with my mouth, "Be alive." To join in one flesh is to say, "I give myself to you in all that this act means," even if my mouth shapes the words, "This means nothing." Now for two persons to give themselves to each other totally is to give what they are *wholly*; what they are *wholly* includes their bodies; and into these bodies is written the potentiality to bring a third person into being. It is part of what they give and receive.

Unitive intimacy, then, is more than intense sexual desire leading to pleasurable intercourse. One condition that makes the mutual gift of selves possible is that the two selves have something to give—that they complement each other. This is possible because there is something missing in the man, which he finds in the woman, and something missing in the woman, which she finds in the man. By themselves, each one is incomplete; to be whole, they must be united. Paradoxically, this incompleteness is a blessing, first because it makes it possible for them to give themselves to each other, and second because it gives them a motive for doing so. The gift of self makes each self to the other what no other self can be. The fact that they "forsake all others" is not just a sentimental feature of traditional Western marriage vows, but arises from the nature of the gift. You cannot partly give yourself, because your self is indivisible; the only way to give yourself is to give yourself entirely. Because the gift is total, and because it joins the very flesh that individuates us, it excludes all others. If it doesn't exclude all others, then it hasn't taken place. What! Have they not had intercourse? Yes, but they used it to lie.[10]

We can say even more about the gift of self. A few moments ago I said that we say things to each other by what our bodies do, In fact, the body is the visible sign by which the invisible self is actually made present and communicates. But if this is true, then the union of the spouses' bodies has a more-than-bodily significance; the body emblematizes the person, and the joining of bodies emblematizes the joining of persons. It is a symbol which participates in, and duplicates the pattern of, the very thing that it symbolizes; one-flesh unity is the body's language for one-life unity.[11]

Nothing else that we do with our bodies is like this. In the case of every other biological power, only one body is required to do the job. A person can digest food by himself, using no other stomach but his own; he can see by himself, using no other eyes but his own; he can walk by himself, using no other legs but his own. So it is with each of the vital functions—except one. The sole exception is procreation. If we were speaking of breathing, it would be as though the man had the diaphragm, the woman the lungs, and they had to come together to take a single breath. If we were speaking of circulation, it would be as though the man had the right atrium and ventricle, the woman the left atrium and ventricle, and they had to come together to make a single beat. Now it isn't like that with the respiratory or circulatory powers, but that is precisely how it is with the procreative powers. The union of complementary opposites is the only possible realization of their procreative potential. Unless they come together as "one flesh"—as a single organism, though with two personalities—procreation doesn't occur.

Why do I spend time on these matters? To emphasize the tightness with which the different strands of our sexual design are woven together. Mutual and total self-giving, strong feelings of attachment, intense pleasure, and the procreation of new life are linked by human nature in a single complex of meanings and purpose. For this reason, if we try to split them apart, we split ourselves. Failure to grasp this fact is more ruinous to our lives, and more difficult to correct, than any amount of ignorance about genital warts. It ought to be taught, but it isn't.

The problem is that we don't want to believe that these things are really joined; we don't want the package deal that they represent. We want to transcend our own nature, like gods. We want to pick and choose among the elements of our sexual design, enjoying just the pieces that we want and not the others. Some people pick and choose one element, others pick and choose another, but they share the illusion that they can pick and choose. Sometimes such picking and choosing is called "having it all." That is precisely what it isn't. A more apt description would be refusing it all—insisting on having just a part—and in the end, not even getting that.

Think of our sexual landscape as a square or quadrant with four corners, A, B, C, and D. Over in corner A are people, mostly men, who buy into the fantasy that they can enjoy greater sexual pleasure by instrumentalizing their partners and refusing the gift of self. By doing so, they fall pell-mell into the hedonistic paradox: Pleasure comes naturally as a by-product of pursuing something else, like the good of another person, and the best way to ruin pleasure is to make it your goal. A rock star of my own generation, now in the ranks of the geezers, used to sing, "I Can't Get No Satisfaction." No one who ever listened to the song imagined that Mick Jagger suffered a shortage of sex. The problem was that all that satisfaction wasn't satisfying anymore. One supposes that it still isn't.

In corner B of the quadrant are other people, mostly women, who try to substitute the mere feelings of union for real union. We catch a hint of how common this is in the debasement of the language of intimacy. In today's talk, "I was intimate with him" means "I had sex with him," no more and no less. This euphemism is used more or less interchangeably with another, "I was physical with him," and that tells you all you need to know. The parties have engaged in a certain transaction with their bodily parts. There may have been one-flesh unity—their bodies may have been acting as a single organism for purposes of procreation—but there has not been one-life unity, because that would require mutual and total self-giving. Even so, the bodily transaction produces feelings of union, because that is what it is designed to produce. Nothing is easier than to confuse these feelings with the thing that they represent and that they are meant to encourage, wondering afterward why everything fell apart. After all, "we felt so close," "we seemed so committed," "we had such a good thing going." Yes, everything except the substance of which the feelings are designed to be a sign.

In corner C of the quadrant are couples who imagine that by denying the procreative meaning of sexuality, they can enhance its unitive meaning. They think that by deliberately avoiding the so-called burden of children, they can somehow enjoy a deeper intimacy. It doesn't work that way. Why should it? The unitive capacities of the spouses don't exist for nothing; they exist for motherhood and fatherhood. That is the matrix in which they develop, for children change us in a way we desperately need to be changed. They wake us up, they wet their diapers, they depend on us utterly. Willy-nilly, they knock us out of our selfish habits and force us to live sacrificially for others; they are the necessary and natural continuation of the shock to our selfishness which is initiated by matrimony itself. By seeking the unity but deliberately refusing the gift of children, we still get a kind of unity, but it goes bad. Because it turns inward, it ferments, turns sour, and begins to stink. The decisive factor is not sterility, which is nobody's fault, but deliberate rejection of fertility. If we willfully refuse the procreative meaning of union, then union itself is stunted. We merely change from a pair of selfish MES to a single selfish US.

In corner D of the quadrant are people who think in exactly the opposite way. Instead of supposing that they can affirm the unitive meaning of sexuality without procreation, they imagine that they can affirm the procreative meaning of sexuality without union. The full shock of this way of life is not with us yet, but our technology already allows it, and in most jurisdictions, so does our law. Meet

Amber, who lives alone, shares social occasions with Dave, in whom she has no sexual interest, and occasionally sleeps with Robert, in whom she has no social interest. Amber wants a child, but she doesn't want the complications of a relationship, and besides, she doesn't want to be pregnant. Where there's a will, there's a way. She contracts with Paul as sperm donor, Danielle as egg donor, Brooke as incubator, and Brian as visiting father figure to provide the child with "quality time." Let us set aside our feelings and attend to what has happened here. Among humans, procreation takes place within the context of a unitive relationship. To destroy the unitive meaning of the procreative act is to turn it into a different act altogether, for it is no longer procreation, but production; the child is no longer an expression of his parents' love, but an output, a product. In simple truth, he has no parents. He was orphaned before his conception. His relation to his caretaker is that of a thing bought and paid for, to the one who bought and paid for it.

Although I have covered a lot of ground in this chapter, I've developed just four themes; allow me to review them. The first is that we need and ought to respect the principles of our sexual design. Just as those ways of living that flout the bodily aspects of our design sicken and kill us, so those ways of living that flout the emotional, intellectual, and spiritual aspects of our design ruin and empty us.

The second theme is that the human sexual powers have meaning and purpose. As the purpose of the visual powers is to see and the purpose of the ingestive powers is to take in nourishment, so the purpose of the sexual powers is to procreate. This purpose is not in the eye of the beholder; apart from this purpose we would have no way to explain why we have them. Moreover, if we try to make use of the sexual powers in ways that thwart and violate this purpose, we thwart and violate ourselves.

The third theme is that the human design for pro-creation requires marital and family life. For guppies, it doesn't; they manage to procreate without them. For us, it does. To put the point another way, we are made with a view to marriage and family, and fitness for them is one of our design criteria. No one invented them, no one is indifferent to them, and there was never a time in human history when they did not exist. Even when disordered, they persist. Spouses and family members who are divided by disaster commonly undertake Herculean efforts to reunite with each other. Marriage and family are not merely apparent goods but real ones, and the rules and habits necessary to their flourishing belong to the natural law.

The final theme is that the spousal bond has its own unitive structure, which nourishes these institutions and is nourished by them in turn. This structure has principles of its own, among them these: Happiness cannot be heightened by sexually using the Other; conjugal joy requires a mutual, total, and exclusive gift of self. Feelings of union are no substitute for union; their purpose is to encourage the reality of which they are merely a foretaste. The procreative and unitive meanings of sexuality are joined by nature; they cannot be severed without distorting or diminishing them both.

These meanings, purposes, and principles are the real reason for the commands and prohibitions contained in traditional sexual morality. Honor your parents. Care for your children. Save sex for marriage. Make marriage fruitful. Be faithful to your spouse.

Let the sexual revolution bury the sexual revolution. Having finished revolving, we arrive back where we started. What your mother—no, what your grandmother—no, what your great-grandmother—told you was right all along. These are the natural laws of sex.

3

The Meaning of
Sexual Differences

All they who serve are telling me
Of Your unnumbered graces;
And all wound me more and more,
And something leaves me dying,
I know not what, of which they are darkly speaking.
　　　　　　　—John of the Cross, *Spiritual Canticle*

How many more colors there are in the world because there are two sexes and not just one! How amusing they are to each other, and yet how baffling! Mutual perplexity can be part of the fun, a fountain of mirth, making the shimmering hues of strangeness sparkle all the more. In our day, though, perplexity isn't so amusing; it has an edge to it. We see all those colors all right, but admitting to the sight is considered shameful and offensive. Just as some ages have held it loutish to work with one's hands, so our time holds it crude to make use of one's eyes. So we make ourselves a little blind. We squint, throw dust in our eyes, and try not to look at things straight on.

A well-socialized young woman whom we may call Carissa had been reading some of the classics for the first time. One day when we were talking, she asked a question which all well-socialized young women who are reading the classics for the first time are expected to ask these days. Why did those bygone writers speak as though men and women are different?

"Maybe because they are different," I said. "Don't you think so?"

Plainly annoyed by my answer, she demanded, "Weren't those old views just prejudices?"

"Well, it's not easy to disentangle the prejudices of one's own time and place from universal truth. Maybe none of those writers did disentangle them perfectly. Still," I said, "aren't certain differences between men and women acknowledged everywhere?"

"But men and women *aren't* different."

"Then why do you think every culture supposes that they are?"

"Oh, I know the sexes *end up* different everywhere," she said. "But that only happens because boys are *raised* differently than girls."

"Let me be sure I follow you. You don't deny that some sex differences are universal—"

"No."

"—but you say they aren't natural. The only reason for them is differences in how boys and girls are brought up."

"That's right."

"Let's think about that. To produce the same differences between boys and girls everywhere, those differences in upbringing would also have to be the same everywhere, wouldn't they?"

"Yes. Boys are *always* raised differently than girls."

"And yet you think these differences in upbringing have no basis in human nature."

"Right, because they don't."

"If they have no basis in human nature, then why are they universal?"

"What do you mean?"

"If they are merely arbitrary, wouldn't you expect them to vary from culture to culture?"

"No, because cultures *influence* each other."

"You mean cultures that raise boys and girls differently influence other cultures to raise them differently?"

"Of course."

"Why shouldn't it be the other way around? If it's all because of culture, then why don't some cultures raise boys and girls the same, and influence other cultures to follow *them*?"

"I don't understand you."

"To put the question another way," I asked, "if the pattern of upbringing has no basis in human nature, then why is it so persistent?"

Carissa dodged the question, instead protesting an opinion I hadn't expressed. "Aren't men and women equally human?"

"Equally human, sure, but not the same. Complementary variations on the same musical theme. Different voices singing in polyphony."

"Tell me *one* fundamental difference between men and women," she demanded.

"That's easy. I could never bear a child. A woman can."

"Not *all* women. Aren't some women infertile?"

"Sure, but you're confusing essence with accident," I said. "A fertile woman can bear a child, but not even a fertile man can pull off a feat like that."

By now Carissa was thoroughly exasperated. Hurling down her trump card, she exclaimed, "I know men's and women's *bodies* are different, but *in their brains* they're just the same."

The details fade from memory, so I may have slightly misquoted some of Carissa's words. Not the words of her final sentence, which have echoed in my mind ever since. This chapter is not about brain science. Nonetheless, let us pause to consider what is known about men's and women's brains.

"In their brains," it turns out, men and women are different after all. According to neuroscientist Larry Cahill, the differences are marked, pervasive, and consistent.[1] The cliché that variation within each sex is greater than variation between the sexes is simply false. Moreover, the contrasts between men and women are evident not just in a few extreme cases, but across the whole distribution, and they involve not only the activity of the brain, but also its organization and development. Doreen Kimura, another brain scientist, remarks that although environment certainly influences us, the differences in brain organization occur "so early in life that from the start the environment is acting on differently wired brains in boys and girls."[2]

How many are these differences in wiring? Legion. To mention just a few: Large parts of the brain cortex are thicker in women than in men. Ratios of gray to white matter vary, too. The hippocampus, which plays a role in memory and spatial navigation, takes up a greater proportion of the female brain than of the male brain. On the other hand, the CA1 region of the hippocampus is larger in the male. A variety of neurotransmitter systems work differently in men and women; neurotransmitters are the chemicals that carry nerve impulses across the synapses. Sex hormones, obviously different in men and women, influence not only the excitability of hippocampus cells, but also various aspects of their structure. The right and left hemispheres are more interconnected in female brains than in male ones, and the corpus callosum, which links them together, is larger. The amygdala, involved in emotion and emotional memory, is larger in men, but the deep limbic system, which is also involved in emotion, is larger in women. Across a spectrum of different functions, which side of the amygdala controls which function is reversed in men and women. Sex-related differences between the hemispheres exist for other brain regions as well, including the prefrontal cortex, involved in personality, cognition, and other executive functions, and the hypothalamus, which links the nervous system with the endocrine system and has some connection with maternal behavior. External circumstances, such as chronic stress, act on male brains differently than on female. Brain diseases also diverge in men and women, not only in their frequency, but in their age of onset, duration, and the way they manifest themselves. Even the neurological aspects of addiction differ between the two sexes.

Although not all neurological differences are associated with behavioral differences, the differences between male and female brains affect numerous aspects of behavior, including "emotion, memory, vision, hearing, processing faces, pain perception, navigation, neurotransmitter levels, stress hormone action on the brain, and disease." Cahill says that "the picture of brain organization that emerges is of two complex mosaics—one male and one female—that are similar in many respects but very different in others. The way that information is processed through the two mosaics, and the behaviors that each produce, could be identical or strikingly different, depending on a host of parameters." He concludes with a quotation from a report of the medical branch of the National Academy of Sciences: "Sex does matter. It matters in ways that we did not expect. Undoubtedly, it matters in ways that we have not yet begun to imagine."[3]

So Carissa had it exactly backwards. It seems that our brains are even more different than the rest of our bodies.

Why is it so hard even to discuss the differences between the sexes? I think because we miss four large truths.

One of these large truths might be called the *duality of nature*. Manhood and womanhood reflect the same human nature, and with equal fidelity and dignity, but they reflect different facets of it. There are two ways to get this matter wrong. One way is to think that because the two sexes are different, they must be unequally valuable—woman an inferior version of man, or man an inferior version of woman. The other way is to think that because the sexes do have equal worth, they must be exactly the same.

Another large truth is the *duality of path*. The developmental trajectories of men and women are different at both ends—not only in what they start with, the susceptibilities and tendencies that each sex must discipline and prune, but in what they end with, what each sex ripens into when all goes as it should. Some people miss the point by ignoring the difference in starting points, as though the difference between the raw materials from which maturity is built were unimportant. That is like thinking that a house can float above its foundations. Others miss the point by paying attention *only* to the difference in starting points. For instance, they may say that men have a stronger desire for sex (which may or may not be true), and then draw the conclusion that a man who beds as many women as possible is more manly than a man who is faithful to his wife (which does not follow).

The third truth is *body and soul unity*. Human beings aren't one thing but two things together, composites of physical body and rational soul, each element equally personal and equally part of what we are. Again there are two opposite ways to miss the mark. One way is to think that the true self is nothing but a body, so that the soul or mind is merely one of its activities, like the secretion of bile.[4] The other way is to think that the true self is nothing but a mind, a non-bodily person mysteriously occupying and using a non-personal body.[5] By the way, readers who are suspicious of religion need not feel jittery about the word "soul." It was used even by the pagan philosopher Aristotle to refer to the formal principle of an embodied human life, the pattern the presence of which makes the difference between a living human body and a human corpse. The pattern "informs" the matter, but is not itself matter. People of my religious tradition would of course say *more* than this about souls, but one who rejects that "more" can still speak of souls. One more thing. "Mind" and "soul" do not mean the same thing. The soul is the pattern of an embodied human life; the mind is one of the powers that this pattern possesses or exercises.

The final large truth is *polaric complementarity*. Men and women aren't just different, but different in corresponding ways. They are complementary opposites—alike in their humanity, but different in ways that make them natural partners. Each sex completes what the other lacks, and helps bring the other into balance. One way to reject this insight is to deny its second element, complementarity, so that the contrast between men and women seems to make them strangers or enemies. The other way to reject the insight is to deny its other element, polarity, so that we can't see the contrast in the first place. Both kinds of denial produce the same result, a kind of solipsism in which each sex views itself as complete and whole just as it is, with no need to be balanced by the other.

I hope it is clear that repudiating any of these four
large truths is asking for trouble. By ignoring the duality of nature, we make it impossible for men and women
to honor each other for what they really are. By failing
to understand the duality of path, we persuade them to
view themselves as either male and female beasts or sexless
angels. By denying body and soul unity, we confuse them
by making their bodily differences seem either irrelevant
or all-important. By denying polaric complementarity, we
undermine their union and destroy their human solidarity.

Where was Carissa in all this? Obviously she denied
the first, second, and fourth large truths—the duality of
nature, the duality of path, and polaric complementarity.
Convinced that any difference between the sexes would
make them unequal, she insisted that they were just the
same. She denied not only the difference in the ore from
which manhood and womanhood are refined, but also the
difference in the steel that results. Finally, her rejection of
the polarity of the two sexes left no room to acknowledge
their mutual need for each other.

Paradoxically, the notion that men and women are
identical works against the very equality that it tries to
uphold. The same, are they? The same as what? Though
with some dissimulation, identicalists almost always
answer, "The same as men." Not only do men who despise
women take this line. It is also taken by those so-called
feminists who detest everything feminine, regard womanly
women as traitors to the cause, and insist on an ideal which
is supposedly indifferent to sex, but is actually masculine.
From the same root spring those strange male fantasies
about worlds of the future in which women lead armies,
command starships, gun down enemies, and are ready for
sexual intercourse at any moment. The underlying wish
is that both sexes would be men, but that some of these

men would look like women. Considering how things have been going lately, I wonder why no one imagines a different future, in which the institution of marriage has disintegrated and women raise children in matriarchal herds, like elephants—the men occasionally drifting to mate, then drifting out to roam with other men. But I digress.

I was saying that Carissa denied the first, third, and fourth large truths. To pick up the thread of the story, it is pretty clear that she denied the second large truth too, body and soul unity, although her remark about the brain was ambiguous. Probably she was an inconsistent materialist, who identified her true self with a part of the body, her brain, while considering the rest of her body beneath notice. But I may be mistaken. She may have been a muddled angelist, who said "brain" although she really meant "mind," and who thought mind is the only thing that matters. Then again she may have viewed her brain as nonbodily, divorced from its material conditions. It is hard to tell.

Perhaps it does not matter much whether she was a materialist or an angelist, because, in an odd way, materialism and angelism leave us equally in suspense. If we are nothing but bodies, then it is difficult to avoid reducing ourselves to our anatomical processes, so that men are but dispersers of seed, women but receptacles and incubators. If we are nothing but minds, then it is difficult to see what our bodies have to do with us at all. On this hypothesis, when a mother kisses her baby, she is not actually kissing, and the baby is not actually being kissed; she is only manipulating her husk, which is not really her, to kiss the baby's husk, which is not really the baby. Some ancient angelists reasoned that since our bodies are not our true selves, we ought to have as little to do with them as possible. In their view, we should be extreme ascetics, regarding even marriage and childbearing as evil. Other angelists reasoned that since our bodies are not our true selves, it makes no difference what we do with them. We may as well be libertines, they thought, and even whoring and dissipation are blameless. None of these views, whether materialist or angelist, makes sense of what we are: ensouled body and embodied soul together, both of them at once.

Why then do we fall for such strange views? Some say, "It's all ideology." That is no answer; what we are asking is why absurd ideologies seem attractive. Others say, "It's all because of disordered family life." That explanation is a little better; when dad flies the coop in order to nest with his secretary, or mom shacks up with her boyfriend, their relationships with their children are certainly thrown into chaos. Should we be surprised if these children carry confused thoughts and resentments about themselves, their parents, and the sexes right into their grown-up life? Wrongheaded sexual ideologies undermine families, and ruined families generate a readiness to accept wrongheaded ideologies. Even so, this answer is not fully satisfying either. There have always been strange ideas and broken families. Why should the vicious circle be especially vicious in our own time? We simply don't know the answer.

But let us leave that aside. Is there a more adequate way to speak about men and women, and a more honest way to understand their differences?

On the assumption that nothing should be taken seriously until it has been counted, some think the path to honesty and clarity lies in the quantitative analysis of cross-cultural psychological surveys. As we paused to consider what men and women look like to brain scientists, let us take time out to consider what they look like to survey researchers.

It turns out that interpreting the results of psychological surveys is more difficult than one might expect. For example, according to one widely used personality assessment, the Myers-Briggs Type Indicator, or MBTI, men are more likely to report a preference for thinking over feeling, women a preference for feeling over thinking.[6] No doubt such a result measures something—but what? It is simply impossible that it could measure what it purports to measure. Why? Because it makes no sense to "prefer" thinking or feeling. Everyone is both feeling and thinking at every moment, and the actions are inseparable. Not even having wandering thoughts is the same as not thinking; not even having calm emotions is the same as not feeling. I cannot say one time, "now I will feel," and at another time, "now I will think." Indeed, what I think affects how I feel, and what I feel affects how I think. If I believe you have cheated me, I will probably feel indignant toward you, and if I feel sympathetic toward you, I will probably try to think of you in the best possible light. Yes, of course, we can integrate feeling with reasoning in different ways. We can even train ourselves to integrate them in one way rather than another. Characteristically, men and women do integrate them differently; it is no accident that men find it easier to feel objectively and women find it easier to think compassionately. But we cannot choose between thinking per se and feeling per se, so there is no sense in asking people, "Which do you prefer?"

Once I offered these reflections to someone who wanted to administer the MBTI to me. She expressed the thought, "That just shows that you prefer thinking to feeling!" I have a clear recollection of experiencing unusually strong feelings about the matter.

Although the MBTI requires impossible choices, most survey researchers try to avoid putting their respondents in such impossible positions. Instead of recording what they say when confronted with a small number of precon-

ceived false alternatives, as in the MBTI, they ask all sorts
of different questions, trying to get at as many personality
traits as possible. Usually they look for patterns of covariation, tendencies for people who have high scores on certain traits to have high scores on other traits, too.[7] What
such research finds is that there are numerous patterned
differences between the sexes. Considering that men and
women belong to the same species and share with each
other the nature of human beings, we would not expect
them to differ significantly on every measure, or even on
most measures, nor do they. In general intelligence, for
example, men differ more from other men, and women differ more from other women, than men and women differ
from each other. But the many sharp differences that do
exist between the sexes hold consistently across countries,
educational levels, ages of respondents, and years in which
the studies are conducted.

Guess what? These differences correspond closely
with traditional views of the differences between men
and women. Not only that, but the differences in views
about the sexes turn out to be just as universal as the differences between the sexes. In other words, not only do
we find the same differences everywhere, but we also
find much the same views *about* these differences everywhere[8]—even in countries like ours, where confessing to
such views is branded as prejudiced and retrograde. Mark
it up as another victory of quantitative social science: We
can now confirm by counting that what everyone used to
know without counting is really true. We can even confirm that although we feign ignorance, some of it is still
really known. How surprising, how unexpected, and—in
the view of some of us—how disturbing.

True, the differences between men and women, taken
as groups, are stronger in some cultures than others. How-

ever, the cross-cultural pattern is not what one would guess. One would expect these differences to be more pronounced in poor, traditionalist countries, and less pronounced in wealthy, individualistic countries. According to Paul T. Costa Jr., Antonio Terracciano, and Robert R. McCrae, they are actually stronger and more pronounced in the latter and less pronounced in the former. No one really knows why. Perhaps the explanation lies in the fact that life is simply harder in poor countries, so that women are more likely to be forced by circumstances to take on unfeminine roles they would rather not assume. Costa, et al., do not consider this hypothesis, but they do take up and reject several others. Their own best guess is that perhaps the survey results have been skewed by differences in how women describe and report their own behavior. In countries where sex roles are strongly emphasized, women may be more likely to say, "this is what one does," while in individualistic cultures, they may be more likely to say, "this is how I am," even though in both cases they are behaving in much the same ways.[9] The jury is still out.

In any case, women everywhere tend to have much higher survey scores than men in nurturance or tender-mindedness, trustfulness, and anxiousness. In various ways, they also show greater sensitivity to emotion. (I hasten to add that this is not the same having a "preference" for emotion over thought—it is really about how feelings are experienced, and how thoughts and feelings interact.) Women experience both positive and negative emotion more strongly and vividly. Moreover, they are more likely to show their emotions in their faces, and they are better at deciphering nonverbal cues about what other people are feeling. Perhaps because of this sensitivity, they are also more vulnerable to moods and mood swings, more likely to show signs of depression, and more susceptible to stress.

On the other hand, they are warmer, more talkative, more gregarious, and more agreeable or compliant. They also differ from men in the way they consider potential mates. In particular, they care much more than men do about ambition and socioeconomic status, somewhat more than men do about intelligence, and somewhat more than men do about moral virtues, like honesty and sincerity.

Men show the opposite patterns. Moreover, on average, they have much higher scores in assertiveness, they are more open to new ideas, and they are more interested in excitement. Some studies suggest that they have higher opinions of themselves: To use the more polite phrase, they have greater self-esteem, and to use the less polite one, greater self-conceit. They also tend to be better at mechanical reasoning and in spatial visualization. In comparing potential mates, they care much more than women do about physical attractiveness. They are also much more likely to engage in sex without personal relationship, a category of behavior which includes both casual and solitary sex.

The fundamental problem with such methods of investigation is that although they accurately measure how men as a group differ from women as a group, they do not really get at the difference between man as such and woman as such. To put the point another way, although they describe numerous differences between men and women, they do not get at the underlying difference, of which all those other differences are mere effects. So-called factor-analytic models, which analyze patterns of covariation in order to reduce large numbers of observed differences to a smaller number of "dimensions" or "factors," are sometimes said to dig deeper. But not even these get down to the underlying causal reality, the essential difference between men and women; they merely describe the effects of that reality in a more efficient and economical way.

Moreover, although such statistical methods are helpful in one way, they are unhelpful in another. If there really is an essential or underlying difference between men and women, then it holds for every man and every woman. Needless to say, the statistical generalizations hold only for some men and women; they are merely averages. Women are in general more talkative, but any given man may be more talkative than most women. Men are in general more assertive, but any given woman may be more assertive than most men. This may be one of the reasons why identicalists like Carissa deny that there is any underlying difference between man as such and woman as such. From their point of view, if you want to describe any given person, Q, you should simply tally Q's various traits. Is Q talkative? Assertive? Tender-minded? Mechanical? Compliant? Once you have done that, you are finished; you know all there is to know. Except for a few purely biological purposes, nothing is added by asking, "Is Q a man or a woman?" True, whether the other person is a man or a woman is the first thing we notice upon meeting. Yet on the identicalist view, that is just one of our quirks. Whether someone is a man or a woman is really unimportant.

There is something odd about this view. If we really believe only in individuals—if we really deny the importance of categories like "man" and "woman"—then why not be consistent? Why stop with sex? Why not apply the same way of thinking to, say, species? If it is true that once you know a person's traits, nothing is added by asking whether he is male or female, then by the same token, shouldn't we say that once you know any being's traits, nothing is added by asking whether it is human or nonhuman? Shouldn't this question be equally unimportant?

As a matter of fact, a fair and increasing number of people do think so. That unimportant question is deeply offensive to them.[10] It generates a feeling of grievance.

Now in order to feel such a grievance, one must view reality in a certain way. I do not say that he must be conscious of viewing it that way; I only say that in order to be offended, he must be viewing it that way. First, he must believe that nothing exists but individual things. In other words, he must take the view that the way that we classify beings is purely arbitrary; "natural kinds" do not exist. He may believe that Mary, Claire, and Felicity are real individuals, but he may not believe that there is any underlying basis in reality for the category "woman." Second, he must view all existing individuals, including individual humans, as just clusters of properties. From this point of view, there isn't anyone deep down whom these properties describe. Claire is simply the sum of qualities like "sings," "has long hair," and "balances her own checkbook." Subtract all these qualities, and there is no Claire; the self who gives rise to these qualities, the subsistent being of whom these qualities are true, does not exist.

Against these two premises I maintain an older view. Individuals are more than just clusters of properties. Human individuals have personal identities; they belong to the natural kind "humanity"; the members of this natural kind are fulfilled in the activities of knowledge, work, and love; and the terms "man" and "woman" express a real division of it. On this account, the difference between men and women is not invented or constructed, but simply recognized. It lies in the nature of things. Yes, of course, cultures try to nuance the difference between men and women in different ways, but that does not make the difference itself just a product of culture. And yes, not all women are more nurturing than all men, not all men are more assertive than all women, and so on. Even so, the fact that *most* women are more nurturing than *most* men is much more than an accident. It arises from a genuine difference in the underlying reality, the difference between woman-hood and manhood as such.

To say that there is a real difference between manhood and womanhood as such is not at all to say that this difference is simple or all-encompassing. Because men and women are not different species, but corresponding sexes of the same species, each is defined partly in terms of the other. When called upon to do so, they can even step outside of their roles in some ways, they can become partners in some of the same tasks, and they can even tone down some of their differences. None of this means they are the same! For even when men and women do step out of their roles, they tend to have different motives for doing so. Even when they do share tasks, they tend to view them differently. And even when they do tone their differences down, the most common reason is that they have taught each other something. How is it that they have something to teach each other? Because they are not the same.

Another aspect of the paradox is that although men and women are capable of the same virtues, they tend to practice them in different modes. Both men and women can be wise, honest, temperate and so on—and they should be. Yet each sex "inflects" the virtues differently.[11] Consider the task of raising good children in a world that threatens to corrupt and unravel them. Because a woman wants to nurture, she conquers her fear of the threat, developing the courage to be a mother. Because a man wants to do hard things, he meets the threat as a challenge, developing the tenderness to be a father. Though she learns courage, her courage is a good deal different from his; though he learns tenderness, his tenderness is a good deal different from hers.

Even more confusing is the fact that men and women are influenced by their masculine and feminine differences even when they defy these differences. From time to time newspapers report cases of young women who have concealed their pregnancies, given birth in secret, then done away with the babies. You will say, "That is not nurturing," and you will be right. Nothing less feminine, nothing more opposed to nurturance, could be imagined. Yet consider *in what ways* these young women do away with their babies. How often they place them in trash cans and dumpsters, still alive! You will say, "That is not nurturing either," and again you will be right. But why don't they just kill them? That is what a man usually does if he wants to do away with a child. Perhaps a young woman imagines her baby resting in the dumpster, quietly and painlessly slipping into a death that is something like sleep. Or perhaps she imagines a fairy tale ending in which someone finds her baby in the dumpster and brings him up as her own. No, the act is not nurturing, but the inclination to nurture hasn't precisely been destroyed; under the influence of other urgent motives, it has been perverted.

I daresay that such data are not captured by our psychological instruments. It is not enough to count things with a survey. One must see with the eyes of the heart.

Perhaps most confusing of all, the underlying realities of the sexes are never perceived *directly*. For that matter, neither is any underlying reality, but for some reason this case seems to puzzle us more. With my eye, I can gaze at any number of women, but all I see is particular women. Not with my eye, but only with my mind, can I see the universal essence, womanhood. Nevertheless, womanhood, like manhood, is real; it is known through its effects. The light of the universal shines through its particular instances, even if only through a fog. Even now, even today, confused and disoriented, the overwhelming majority of men do not think of themselves simply as Frank, Steven, or Abdul.

They think of themselves as men, and want to be recognized as masculine. Nor do the overwhelming majority of women think of themselves simply as Mary, Claire, or Felicity. They think of themselves as women, and want to be recognized as feminine.

If we do need to appeal to underlying causal realities, why not just say "DNA"? Because even though our bodies are truly part of us, we are more than bodies. Our DNA is not simply what we are, any more than our eye colors, bone densities, or brain mosaics are what we are. Then is our DNA irrelevant to what we are? Not that either. Just as a song, a love story, or even a flawed book like this speaks to our minds about what we are, perhaps the information encoded in our DNA speaks to our flesh about what we are. Flesh holds converse with flesh, mind holds converse with mind, and mind holds converse with body.

But this raises another question. I said that the light of essential manhood and womanhood shines out, but only through a fog. How can that fog be dispersed? How can the realities of manhood and womanhood be conveyed to minds like ours, which have such difficulty seeing them? How can they penetrate eyelids that are almost squinted shut?

Would it be possible to break through simply by defining the two sexes? Would that be too simple? One never knows until one tries, so let us try.

Then again, people have different ideas about definition. One supposed method of definition is to break things down into simpler parts and then put them back together. For example, I might say that a watch has a spring, a dial, two hands, and a variety of other pieces, connected in a certain way. Such information is nothing to sneeze at; it is useful for watchmakers. However, it is not what I am calling a definition, because it doesn't tell us what a watch actually is. Still less can such an approach tell us what a man or woman is. I might correctly point out that a woman normally has a head, limbs, and a variety of other organs, all connected in a certain way. But so much might also be true of a woman's corpse, and this doesn't tell us the difference between a woman and her corpse. Nor does that kind of information make sense of the fact that a woman who is missing a part, say one of her arms, is still entirely a woman. At most, such information describes a woman's body. But she is more than a body; the personal reality that is she has an immaterial aspect as well. Very well, can we break down this immaterial aspect into parts, as we break down the body? I don't think so. Does it even make sense to speak of souls as having parts? Her brain has various parts, but that is not the same thing. Her immaterial soul has various immaterial powers, such as reason, memory, and imagination, but powers are not parts; they are not portions of her self, or divisions of her self, but capacities that are exercised by her one and undivided self. Besides, she shares all these powers with men. Don't they too have reason, memory, and imagination?

Is there then a better way to define things? There is. Consider the watch again. Instead of breaking it down and putting it back together, we can say that it is a machine for telling time. This sort of definition explains what watches are by relating them to other kinds of things. It identifies the broad category to which they belong, machines, along with the essential characteristic that distinguishes them from other machines, the fact that they are used for telling time.

Can we define womanhood in that way? We can. We can say that a woman is a human being of that sex whose members are potentially mothers. The broad category here is human beings; an essential characteristic that distinguishes some human beings from others is the potentiality for motherhood. So let us begin here.

I say "begin here," rather than "end here," in part because the idea of "potentiality for motherhood" needs explanation. One reason is that potentiality is often confused with physical possibility. Consider a woman who is infertile. Perhaps, by mischance, an infection has scarred her fallopian tubes. Although it is physically impossible for her to be a mother, we should not say that she lacks the potentiality for motherhood. She has that potentiality as a woman, even though her potentiality cannot be physically realized because of the scarring. It is just because she is a real woman, just because she is naturally endowed with the potentiality for motherhood, that the block to the physical realization of the potentiality is such a loss to her, such an occasion for sorrow.

Another reason why the expression "potentiality for motherhood" requires explanation is that although bearing children is the most characteristic expression of motherhood, it is far from its only expression. A woman might even physically bear a child yet fail in the greater perspective of motherhood, because after she carries the child in her womb and brings him into the world, she neglects him; she fails to nurture him with that mother's love which only she can give because it is different from a father's love. When I speak of such failure, by the way, I am not speaking of giving up a child for adoption. In some cases such an act may be profoundly maternal, for if a mother is unable to raise her child, then it is an act of sacrificial love to give her child up to a woman who can. My point is that potentiality for motherhood includes more than potentiality to give birth. That is why the woman who accepts the child is in that respect a true mother, too.

We can carry this line of reasoning still further. A potentiality is something like a calling. It wants, so to speak, to develop; it demands, so to speak, a response. Of course this is figurative language, because a potentiality has no will of its own. Yet it really is directed to fruition. The potentiality for motherhood is like an arrow, cocked in the string and aimed at the target, even if it never takes flight. It intimates an inbuilt meaning, and expresses an inbuilt purpose, which cannot help but influence the mind and will of every person imbued with them. A woman may be unaware of this secret influence, and she may even fight against it. But she cannot destroy it. This is why Alice von Hildebrand has remarked that even though not every woman is called to marry and bear physical children, "every woman, whether married or unmarried, is called upon to be a biological, psychological or spiritual mother." A woman knows intuitively, von Hildebrand insists, the profound importance of caring for others, suffering with and for them, "for maternity implies suffering."[12] Although this knowledge is intuitive, in a well-functioning society it is deepened and made explicit by the traditions that mothers pass on to their daughters, generation by generation.

Obviously I cannot speak from inside experience of womanhood, because I am a man. Yet even a man can see that it is a very different thing to be a woman than to be a man. This is true at every stage of life, but it is especially true in the childbearing stage. What women say about themselves confirms my judgment. A man may deeply love his child, but he has not carried the child in his body for nine months before his birth, or nourished the child with milk from his breasts. These experiences connect the mother with her child in an intimate, physical bond which we men can easily recognize, but which we cannot experience. In subtle ways they condition her emotional responses not only toward the child, but also toward herself and even toward everyone else. They also make sense of certain other differences between men and women, differences for which women are sometimes wrongly criticized. For example, are women in general more conscious of their bodies than men are? Of course they are. Are they more protective of themselves physically than men are? Yes, certainly. But considering their potentiality for motherhood, this heightened physical awareness is entirely appropriate. It may present temptations to vanity, yes, but in itself it is not vain, and to cowardice, yes, but it is not cowardly. Women need to be like this. There would be something wrong if they were not like this. Men, by being men, are not more virtuous; their most characteristic temptations are merely somewhat different from a woman's, and their virtues have different inflections.

The other sexual differences make sense in this light, too. As Edith Stein reminds us,[13] men are more prone to abstraction, and women more prone to focus on the concrete. Men don't mind what is impersonal; women are more attuned to the nuances of relationships, and to what is going on in other people. A man tends to be a specialist and single-tasker; he develops certain qualities to an unusually high pitch, using them to do things in the world. A woman tends to be a generalist and multitasker; she inclines to a more rounded development of her abilities, using them to nurture the life around her. The woman's potentiality for motherhood ties all her qualities together and makes sense of her contrast with men. Consider just that multitasking capacity. In view of what it takes to run a home, doesn't it make sense for her to have it? A woman must be a center of peace for her family, even though a hundred things are happening at once.

Although men gravitate to careers and women to motherhood, not all women will pursue an exclusively domestic life. Even so, the potentiality for motherhood explains why women who do pursue a career, and who have free choice of career, tend to choose careers that allow them to give the first place to caring for their children. It also explains why they tend to choose careers that give greater scope to maternal qualities. Let us not forget that well-balanced women who do choose traditionally masculine careers also tend to perform them in ways that give scope to maternal qualities. A male lawyer tends to focus on the properties of the task itself. This is worthy, but it is all too easy for him to lose sight of the humanity of his clients. Can he learn to remind himself their humanity? Of course he can, but he is more likely to need the reminder in the first place. A female lawyer may find the abstract quality of the law, which is necessary, somewhat alienating. On the other hand, she is much less likely to forget that she is dealing with human beings.

A quick caveat before going on: The things I have just written are true only when women are allowed to be themselves. Under the spell of identicalism, they may not be allowed to be themselves. If they are punished for their feminine qualities, or if they self-censor them in order to beat men at their own game, they may think they don't want to be themselves. Feminism has brought about a terrible fear and hatred of everything womanly.

These few paragraphs about womanhood may have given the impression that men are to be defined negatively. Someone reading them might suppose that if a woman is a human being of that sex whose members have the potentiality for motherhood, then a man is simply a human being of the sex whose members *lack* the potentiality for motherhood—making the man a sort of incomplete woman. On the contrary! A man, like a woman, is correctly defined only when he is positively defined. He is a human being of the sex whose members have a *different* potentiality than women do: the potentiality for fatherhood. Just as motherhood is broader than biological motherhood, so fatherhood is broader than biological fatherhood. Just as not all women are called to marry and bear children, so not all men are called to marry and sire children. Yet just as all women are called to motherhood in a larger sense, so we may say that all men are called to fatherhood in a larger sense. And just as extended motherhood is well understood only when motherhood as such is well honored, so extended fatherhood is well understood only when fatherhood as such is well honored.

I say this in earnest, yet it is much more difficult to speak about fatherhood than motherhood. Perhaps because the father's connection with his children is not mediated by his body in the way that the mother's is—or perhaps because paternal absenteeism and other forms of masculine failure are so conspicuous in our day—most of us have a dimmer idea of fatherhood than motherhood. Open mockery of fathers has become a fixture of popular culture.

The difference between fatherhood and motherhood, hence between manhood and womanhood, involves a difference in the male and female modes of love for their children, but there is much more to it than that. The difference is both greater and deeper. Manhood in general is outward-directed, and womanhood inward-directed. This is no cliché; the distinction is quite subtle. Outward-directedness, for example, is not the same as *other*-directedness, for many men prefer dealing with things. Inward-directedness is not same as *self*-directedness, for the genius of women includes caring for the local circle. If the contrast between outward- and inward-directedness sounds like a dig at male vanity or sexual promiscuity, or for that matter at female narcissism or emotional dependency, it isn't that either. Characteristics of those sorts are not the essence of the sexual difference; they are merely vices that result from the indulgence of

temptations to which the two sexes are unequally susceptible. In speaking of outward- and inward-directedness, my
intention is not to call attention to the corruptions, but to
the good things that are sometimes corrupted. It is a good
thing that an unmarried man pursues the beloved, whereas
an unmarried woman makes herself attractive to pursuit;
that a husband protects the home, whereas a wife estab-
lishes it on the hearth; that a father represents the family
and oversees it, whereas a mother conducts the family and
manages it.

Although the directive geniuses of the father and the
mother are not the same, both of them truly rule the home.
We may compare the father with a king reigning over a
commonwealth, the mother with a queen. These potent
archetypes express nobility, glory, and self-command. Men
joke about their wives telling them what to do. The joke
would have no point unless two things were true: On one
hand, they would not want their wives to be kings; on the
other hand, they know they are really queens. It would
not be absurd to suggest yet another analogy. The father
and mother share and divide the different aspects of sovereignty between themselves in much the same way that
the directive functions are divided in corporations. Does
this seem to be a new idea, an accommodation to current
fashion? Far from it. In a first-century letter from one of
our oldest wisdom writers, St. Paul, to a young man he is
grooming for leadership, we find him using a curious pair
of words—a verb, *proistemi*, and a noun, *oikodespotes*—
one of them for what a husband characteristically *does,* the
other what a wife characteristically *is.* Both words indicate
authority. The former has a range of meanings that include
standing before, presiding, superintending, protecting,
maintaining, helping, succoring, and acting in the capacity
of a patron—very much like a chairman of the board. But

the latter means "ruler of the house"—very much like the chief executive officer. So the idea is really very ancient.[14]

When all goes well, fathers and mothers also exemplify and specialize in different aspects of wisdom. A wise father teaches his wife and family that in order to love you must be strong; a wise mother teaches her husband and family that in order to be strong you must love. She knows that even boldness needs humility; he knows that even humility needs to be bold. He is an animate symbol to his children of that justice which is tempered by mercy, she a living emblem of that mercy which is tempered by justice. Each of them refracts a different hue from the glowing light of royalty. A wise father knows when to say, "ask your mother," a wise mother when to say, "ask your father." When they do this, they are not passing the buck, but sharing sovereignty.

Today it is almost embarrassing to read prose like the patch I have just written. Comparisons of fathers and mothers with kings and queens seem naïve, sentimental, and exaggerated. They make us squirm. There are strong reasons for this reaction, but they are bad ones. How many parents have lost their regal dignity, disbelieve in their authority, and confuse the proper humility of their office with being self-mocking and ironic? We have turned husbands and wives into androgynous "spouses," fathers and mothers into interchangeable "parent figures." We approach having a child like acquiring a pool table or wide-screen TV. Would it be fun? Would it be tedious? Would it be worth the expense? Fathers and mothers have need of recovering their sense of regal calling, taking up their ball and scepter, and ruling their dominions with love for their precious subjects. It is not for nothing that the king of a commonwealth is called "Sire"; humanly speaking, of the callings of fatherhood and kingship, the deeper and more primordial is fatherhood.

May it be needless to say that mothers and fathers must also recover the conviction of their need for each other. This they must do not only for their own sakes, but for their young. Every child needs both a mother's and a father's love. It is not enough to provide an intermediate love that is half motherly and half fatherly, or an inconsistent love that is motherly at some times, fatherly at others. Nor is it enough to give one kind of love for real, while giving only a pretense or simulacrum of the other kind. Even though the two loves resemble each other, they are distinct, and neither can be imitated by anything else. It may be true heroism when through no fault of one's own, a father or a mother raises a child all alone; yet it is better not to be alone. No woman can fully take the place of a father, nor can any man substitute for a mother.[15]

Though I have been speaking of fatherhood and motherhood in relation to the family, these matters actually reach much further. For men, growing up is like joining a brotherhood. Our grasp on this fact is attenuated by the fact that we have lost our rites and customs of apprenticeship and coming of age. Men naturally desire to be something like knights, who not only do hard things, but in firm and fatherly manner train squires who attend them so that these young men can learn to do hard things, too. As I was in earnest before, about the calling of all men to extended fatherhood, so I am in earnest now, about the chivalric element in this calling. A man will more readily aspire to manhood if he can taste it; his life must have the flavor of valor. This is true of how he carries himself not only toward other men, but toward women. The fashion of the day is to think of medieval knights not as valiant but as cruel. Many were, yet even in that day, knighthood was more than a veneer for oppression. It was a great and noble ideal that did much to civilize a society still governed by a warrior caste and too often running with blood. Like the members of our own ruling class, different as it is, the members of that caste sometimes fought for the wrong things, fought in the wrong ways, or committed atrocities. All such perversions should be condemned. Yet let us not abuse the members of that caste just because they liked to fight. Are there not plenty of things to fight for in this world, and plenty of evils to oppose?

After all, most men do not *simply* like to fight; they are too lazy for that. They like to fight when there is something worth fighting for. True, they sometimes make up things worth fighting for just to be able to fight for them, and one of the tasks of becoming a man is learning to resist the temptation. Yet there are plenty of noble things to fight for without making them up. One must war against temptation, capture the citadel of virtue, contend for just laws, defend and protect sound traditions, attack lies and fallacies with the weapons of frankness and reason, and even, yes, make gentle war for courtesy. By the way, if it is right at times to fight, then it is also right to enjoy fighting, even though it is also right to grieve the evils incidental to the struggle and to try to minimize them. A certain militancy and a certain vigilance are essential parts of manhood, and a man's great project is not to do away with his impulse to fight, but to learn to fight nobly and generously—to refine the raw ore, burn away its dross, and make it into purified steel.

This is an ideal to which any man may aspire. It is wholly independent of what he does for a living, of how much education he has had, or of whether he is muscular or athletic. Medieval knights engaged their enemies physically, and there is always some need for that; in our time we have armies and police. Yet there are many ways to fight besides the physical. One may fight through a word in season, a clap on the shoulder, a quiet admonishment or commendation. One may wage war by bearing witness, by lifting the fallen, by refusing to countenance evil. One may do battle by admonishing idlers, by encouraging the faint-hearted, by helping the weak.

Unlike the achievement of biological maturity, the achievement of manhood is hard work, labor that requires a firm hand with the desires and devices of the heart. Alas that the carving and shaping of these impulses is so unfashionable. We have not yet got over teachers like Freud, who called such noble woodcraft "repression," considering it, though necessary, unnatural. His doctrine was deluded and false, because the nature of a thing is set not by its beginning but its end; the fact that our impulses resist being carved and shaped takes away nothing from the fact that they need all that carving and shaping to real-ize their inbuilt purposes. The truth is that *not* to endure being carved and shaped well is unnatural, and a source of numberless miseries. The best instance of an oak is not a gaudily decorated acorn, but a tree; in the same way, the best instance of a human male is not a glorified, walking packet of urges, but a man who, for the sake of the high-est and greatest goods, commands himself, strengthens his brothers, and defends his sisters, regarding even the mean-est of women as a lady.

Once upon a time the differences between men and women were not thought so strange. We have a long quest and a difficult journey before we can speak of them again with ease and gaiety. There are so many sweet and lovely things that our ears can no longer hear without odium, so many blameless things that can hardly be discussed with-out scandal. Just imagine the din that would erupt if I were to praise and extol that great activity that comes so much more readily to the woman, and is slandered under the false name of passivity: *Fiat mihi secundum verbum tuum!*

And if I were to compound the offense by pointing out that every last one of us, both man and woman, is feminine with respect to—but I have promised not to speak of that yet, and I will keep my vow.

When we do attempt the journey back to the commonwealth of sense, we will meet trolls and enchanters on the way. They will obstruct passage, demand tribute, and try to lure us into byways and bogs. But why should that discourage us? We are already begrimed and bewitched. The first thing to do is open our eyes, grasp hold of the nearest branches, and pull ourselves out of the ooze. Odd knights we! Having made ourselves muddy and ridiculous, we may as well journey with a smile.

4

The Meaning
of Sexual Love

There He gave me His breasts,
There He taught me the science full of sweetness.
And there I gave to Him
Myself without reserve;
There I promised to be His bride.
                    —John of the Cross, *Spiritual Canticle*

This chapter is a bit more difficult than the previous ones, and I apologize for that. Isn't love supposed to be easy? One of the hits of my own generation said so. It's a golden song for singing in the shower. The singer croons that he "don't know much" about history, biology, "a science book," or "the French I took"—

But I do know that I love you
And I know that if you love me too
What a wonderful world this would be.[1]

There you have it. The liberal arts and natural sciences are hard, but love is easy, and it makes everything all right.

That's not all wrong. Falling in love is easy. But practicing it is hard. Understanding it is harder yet, because we mean more than one thing by "love."

Another difficulty of the subject is scandal. I am going to connect love with marriage, but today the suggestion that the two things are linked is considered quite a bit over the top. A generation ago, that notion had already come to be viewed as quaint. Just a few years later, it was viewed as rigid. Now it is coming to be seen as a little bit indecent. We are supposed to believe that although love and marriage may happen to coincide, they have no essential affinity with each other. Love happens without marriage, marriage without love, love with various sorts of makeshift arrangement that may or may not imitate marriage; love with marriage may be one of the possibilities, we concede, but surely it is the most awkward, confining, and implausible—isn't it? If someone suggests that the facts may be otherwise, he is met with offended disbelief. What's his problem? Is he just narrow-minded, or something worse?

But I do suggest that the facts are otherwise. "It is in the nature of love to bind itself";[2] vows are love's native language. Love that is mute in the language of promises, though it may be called love, is not love but something else. Even the medieval courtly lovers, who glamorized the love of women not their wives, paid backhanded homage to the fact, for they delighted in extravagant vows. Those few of them who really understood what they were doing made a vow almost as extravagant as the marriage vow itself: to love their lovers chastely. Compared with these great fools, we moderns are pikers. Our foolishness is of the more clownish variety that says, "I have a committed relationship," even though the whole point of the relationship is avoiding commitment.

In a previous chapter I mentioned a young man who still wanted to commit himself, to bind his will. He told me that he longed to get married and stay married to the same woman forever. Yet because his own parents hadn't managed it, he despaired. From my remarks about promises, you might expect a cheap dismissal: "He must not have been in love." That would miss the point, because he didn't claim to be in love. He only claimed that he wanted to love, that he wanted to make promises—and I believed him. Nevertheless, he feared love.

If he was a coward—as in some sense he was—at least his cowardice was high-minded. The thought that provoked him to despair wasn't that his wife might turn out to be a shrew, but that he might turn out to be a heel. He knew love longs to bind itself, but he also believed that it is in the nature of bound things to come unraveled. He knew love longs to make promises, but he also feared that it is in the nature of the heart to soil and trample them.

Marriage rests on a different and more radical supposition: that promises can be kept. In fact, it rests on a supposition more startling still, for traditionally, not only do the lovers make various promises that spring from love, they promise love itself. From the instant of pledging till the parting by death, they vow to love and cherish. Even more pointedly, they promise this love not only if things work out, but even if they don't: "For better, for worse, for richer, for poorer, in sickness and in health."

It is certainly realistic to admit that things might not work out, but how can it be realistic to promise love anyway? If sexual love is what we commonly take it to be, then how can it be promised even if things do work out? One cannot promise to have feelings; one cannot even promise to have sexual feelings. "I, Denny, promise you, Sheila, always to feel a certain minimum level of amorous stimulation in your presence." Impossible.

But let us replace this with a different question. If sexual love is something that can be promised, then what can it be?

Getting the answer right depends on distinguishing between different aspects of sexual love. There is an aspect that can be promised, and there is another that cannot. But we must start even further back than that with another kind of love, the kind called charity. We have then not only two things to discuss, but three.

Charity is an attitude that exults in the sheer existence of the other person. In the words of Josef Pieper, it wants to say, "It is good that you exist; it is good that you are in this world!" Pieper remarks that it is not primarily a condition of the feelings but an attitude of the will: "I *want* you to exist!"[3]

Since charity lies in the will, it might also be put: "I am prepared to do something about it!" Is it accompanied by feelings? No doubt it is, though not always by the same ones. But *is* it a pleasant feeling? No. So far is charity from being a pleasant feeling that I may have charity for you even if I have unpleasant feelings about you. I may think it is good that you exist, I may want you to exist, and I may be prepared to do something about it, even though you have become a source of manifold sorrow to me. I would rather be unhappy about you, than happy without you in the world.

Consider the implications. If I delight in your existence, then I must want something more for you than just your existence, must I not? The attitude we are speaking of does not say, "It is good that you exist, so that you may suffer!" If I delight in the good that you are, then I must want you to experience all the good that you can: "I want you to exist well and beautifully!" So charity entails a permanent commitment of the will to the true good of the other person. I want you to be and to live, I want good things for you, I want to do good things to you, I even want to do good things because of you. Good itself seems better because of you.

Moreover, because charity is not a feeling but an activity of the will, it is something that one decides to do, and it can be promised. I can vow never to despair that you exist, but always to go on wanting you to exist. I can promise that from this day forward, I shall continue to will your true good. I can vow to learn the practices and disciplines that such a will entails. I can vow to have this will even if our friendship is strained—if at this minute I find it difficult to enjoy your company or see eye to eye with you. To be sure, such love costs me something, makes me spend myself, even makes me *want* to spend myself. But there is something strange about such spending. In its perfection, the person whom I love becomes another self to me. Even though I forget myself, I am not diminished by the forgetting. I lose myself, only to find myself in a more spacious continent. "Love never ends."[4] If the will is unwilling to be bound, what we have is not charity, but a passing good feeling.

Let us not be mistaken here: There is nothing erotic about charity in itself. I can have charity for parents, for children, for friends, for comrades yoked in a common task; these are not erotic loves. What I am saying is that just as charity can be practiced in those contexts, so it can be practiced in the context of eros.

Here arises a paradox that gives rise to endless confusion. Let us creep up on it slowly. Start with the observation that in itself, charity is not logically limited to one object. The only logical limit on self-giving in general is that I cannot give more than I am, I cannot spend more than I have. Someone might say this isn't true—that although I can spend parts of myself for many people, I can spend my whole self for one person only; after all, once I yield everything, there is nothing left to yield. On the contrary, a person can certainly give his whole life for many at once, for example when a soldier throws himself on a grenade to save his buddies.

The paradox is that although charity in general is not limited to a single object, erotic charity is. Not only does it suffer such a limitation, it delights in it: "I am my beloved's and my beloved is mine."[5] This puzzling fact requires explanation.

Before delving into the paradox we must be sure what we are talking about. Charity in general is a permanent commitment of the will to the true good of another person; erotic charity is a mode of this will, particularized toward a single person of the polar, complementary sex, and consummated by the joining of their bodies into one. Now in one sense, all charity is expressed by the body, though obviously not all charity is expressed in the distinctively erotic way. In fact, all human action and relationship whatsoever is mediated by the body. This flesh, which we can see and touch, is the emblem, the vesture, the raiment of the soul, which we can neither see nor touch. It is the vehicle through which the soul acts, the means by which it makes itself known, the channel through which it communes with other souls. Only through our bodies do we have knowledge of other persons at all. Parents know their infants through the way they wriggle their torsos, coo with their lips, and give off the scent of babies. Furniture movers know their partners through the placement and exertion of their limbs, the shifting of the load, and the sweat and smell of the labor. Friends say they know each other's minds, and so they do; but they know them through the muscles which give expression to their faces, the lungs which project their breath, and the cords in their throats which modulate that breath into words. From time immemorial, one of the meanings of the word "person" has been simply "body," for although we are more than bodies, we are never less than bodies.

Just in the sense that erotic charity is expressed through the body, then, it is no different than charity in general. It is a bodily act to encourage a friend, to teach a class, to give a cup of water to a thirsty stranger, to carry in the groceries for an elderly neighbor. The distinctive thing about sexual love is that it desires the *joining* of polar, corresponding bodies; in the ancient phrase, the two become one flesh. This difference sets sexual love profoundly apart from all other loves, because our bodies are what individuate us. You and I are equally human, yet we distinguish me, as this human, from you, as that human, through the difference in our matter, bodies, flesh. I don't mean that we don't have other differences, too. What I mean is that ultimately, all of the other differences between us are known and experienced through that one. The flesh is a sign, but also more than a sign. It is not just that which stands for the soul, but that through which the soul is incarnate in the world.

Consequently, though all charity is a gift of self in the general sense that I spend myself, the joining of polar, corresponding bodies is a gift of self in a particular way, a way that no other such gift can be, because it is a fusing, a joining, a union of the very matter that *makes* us different selves. Any other gift of self can be made to any number of persons, but this gift of self picks out one person from the multitude and makes my body hers. Bone cries to bone and flesh cries to flesh, "Here at last is bone of my bone and flesh of my flesh; I give myself to you and to no other!" By the way, this is the reason why, even in a culture that views sexual jealousy as silly, sexual jealousy persists. After all my fashionable joinings and severings, rejoinings and reseverings, when I have turned myself into a mass of erotic scar tissue, when at last all feeling has faded from the many-times-amputated stump, even then I may suffer the painful sense of connection to an absent lover, like the phenomenon of phantom limb.

One more point before we go on. Following greater teachers, I have described erotic charity as a gift, a donation, of the self. It may be said that to give myself is wrong. If I give myself to another, am I not turning myself over to be exploited? Am I not giving someone else the permission to use me like a tool? The answer is no; but why? Certainly the objection must be taken seriously. The fear that drives it is that to give myself is to give myself *away*. Let us then ask the question: Are giving and giving away always the same? Everyday experience shows us that although they are the same in the case of some kinds of gift, in the case of others they are different. If I give you money, yes, I have given it away; your gain is my loss. But if I give you knowledge, I have not given it away at all; I possess what I have given as fully as before. We see then that as there are different kinds of gifts, there are different kinds of giving. Now consider the gift of self. Is it the kind that is giving away, or the kind that isn't?

Consider. What I am giving is what I am; what I am is a person. If by giving myself to you, I ceased to be what I am, then the gift would not actually have occurred; it would have been like a Christmas present that vanished the moment it was opened. Conversely, for the gift to take place, I must be just as much a person after the gift as before, except that now you enjoy my person, too. But what is it that I am giving—what is a person? A person is "what is most perfect in all nature"[6]—a complete individual reality, existing in itself, different from all other somethings, made for rationality, the ultimate possessor under God of all it is and does. A person is not a thing to be owned, a thing to be used, or a *thing* of any sort at all; it is by nature the very kind of being that must not be treated as a thing. I cannot give you permission to exploit me, because I am not the source of what I am, and I cannot make myself a different kind of being than I am, a kind that may be treated as a thing. That is simply not in my power. Neither would it be in your power to give me permission to exploit you. If you and I do give ourselves to each other, then what we receive from each other are not tools, but the opposite of tools. We receive each other, not to be used, but to be cherished. By the gift, we are not shrunken, but enlarged.

To review the ground that we have traveled so far, I have defined charity, and I have described erotic charity. Erotic charity is the aspect of sexual love that can be promised. The aspect of sexual love that *cannot* be promised is our next topic, romantic love. A map may help us to understand the territory.

On the left we have three nested ovals. The biggest one is charity; nothing but charity is truly worth the name

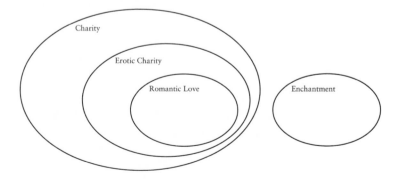

of love. Erotic charity is a mode of charity, and in turn, romantic love is a mode of erotic charity. For greater precision, I might have called romantic love "romantic charity," but that would sound odd, and I prefer to use a familiar term when one is available. The expression "erotic charity" supplies quite enough oddity for one day.

Not all who are "in" erotic charity experience their love in the romantic mode. That doesn't make it false or unworthy. On the other hand, romantic love does have certain desirable elements—along with certain perils, as all real goods do. Enchantment, the little oval to the right, is not a mode of love, but an emotional experience that is often confused with one. One can "fall into" enchantment, just as one can "fall into" romantic love, but they are not the same thing.

Enchantment is the lovely emotional infatuation in which a particular man and a particular woman can't get enough of each other. I could almost define romantic love as the mode of erotic charity of which enchantment is the imitation. The difference is that enchantment is a matter of the feelings, while romantic love, like all charity, is an attitude of the will. Enchantment imitates romantic love in at least two ways. One is that the feelings of the two people may prompt them to do nice things for each other, at least while the feelings last. The other is that if the feelings do last long enough, the doing of nice things might to some degree become habitual—in other words, the two people may fall into genuine charity, the real thing. In itself, however, enchantment is ephemeral. Yes, the man and woman *feel* wonderful about each other's existence, but the feelings may go away.

Other people fall into a closely related mistake. Just because enchantment sometimes precedes charity, they take enchantment to be a necessary first phase of romantic love—something that gradually fades and is replaced by erotic charity if all goes well. The grain of truth here is that enchantment *may* be replaced by erotic charity if all goes well. Even so, the first-phase theory is misleading. One reason is that men and women may pass through many enchantments without ever passing on to erotic charity. The other is that they may go straight into erotic charity *without* first passing through enchantment. By overlooking these two facts, multitudes of people come to pain. Some couples, well on the way to erotic charity, worry unnecessarily, thinking that just because they don't feel enchantment, there must be something wrong with them or they must not be right for each other. Other couples, *not* on the way to erotic charity, mistakenly think that just because they do feel enchantment, they *must* be right for each other. Consequently, people end some relationships needlessly, and dig themselves into others that should end.

Although romantic love is a genuine mode of erotic charity, not all true lovers experience it. Culture has something but not everything to do with the matter, for although romantic love is a permanent human possibility, some people are just not susceptible. It is a requirement of love that the lovers have erotic charity, but it is not a requirement of erotic charity that they be romantic. There is nothing they can do to force themselves to be romantic, and their love is not diminished just because they don't hear it in the romantic key. On the other hand, if they do have erotic charity, their love may come to be romantic, even if it didn't begin in that way.

It is one thing to distinguish romantic love from enchantment, but it is another to try to describe it; one thing to say what it isn't, another to say what it is. One thing that makes the task difficult is that feelings and volitions weave in and out of each other, and even though romantic love is fundamentally an attitude of the will, it is difficult to describe it without borrowing from the language of emotion. Another difficulty is that romantic love has various "moments" or elements. I don't want to make too much of these difficulties. It isn't as though we were speaking of something like quantum chromodynamics, which most people know nothing about; the moments of romantic love are matters of common experience. Even so, an ordinary person can experience a great deal without grasping what it means—even without noticing that it is happening. Experience does not interpret itself. A good deal of ancient civilizational wisdom has been built up to help us out, but in our time, we have dismissed most of it. We think we know better.

Contrary to common opinion, even though the different moments of romantic love are aspects of the same process in the soul, they do not necessarily occur together. Nor, so far as I can see, do they occur in any particular order; though I call them "moments," they are not chronological moments, or stages of development.[7] Contrary to another common opinion, the natural habitat of romantic love isn't the fly-me-to-the-moon escapade, but humdrum matrimony. So far is the married state from putting an end to romantic love that for many people, the first experience of it comes only after they have been married a long time and are well-practiced in charity. Often romantic love catches them by surprise, especially if they have never passed through enchantment, or if they passed through it once, but it cooled. Perhaps they have been going about the everyday business of loving each other for years—and now this celestial gleam! Another quirk of romantic love is that a given man and woman do not necessarily experience the same moments of it, or at the same time, or in the same order. Considering the polaric complementarity of man and woman, that sort of coincidence is probably rare.

The continent of romantic love is immense. Since we have time only for a fly-over, I will point out just eight of its moments. Four may be called Dantean, because they are so beautifully illustrated by the opening pages of *La Vita Nuova,* a work by Dante Alighieri about his love for the Florentine girl Beatrice. The other four are brought exquisitely into focus by an ancient Hebrew poem, the Song of Songs, in which a young woman of lower class, called only "the Shulammite," intrepidly spurns the advances of the king, preferring her shepherd lover "who pastures his flock among the lilies."[8] We may call these moments Shulammitic.

Here begins the new life. Dante wrote, "In the book of my memory, after the first pages, which are almost blank, there is a section headed *Incipit vita nova,* 'Here begins the new life.'"[9] Though perhaps not as dramatically as in Dante's case, such is the experience of all romantic love. It is not a new phase of life, but a new life altogether, as though the lover were a newborn person, beginning again.

Dante, the classic case of the man struck by lightning, perceived the new life all at once. For most lovers, the new life announces itself more gradually, like the whisper of wind at fresh dawn. The sense of its newness deepens; the longer it endures, the newer it is. This new life may not even be noticed while it is coming to be. Its arrival may be seen only in retrospect, after it has come. The memory of life before love becomes dimmer; waking life seems to begin with the beloved. We see then that what is most eminently true of divine love[10] is true in some measure of all romantic love: One must be born again. New birth has as its corollary that there must be a death.

The death of the old life is as real as any death, for one cannot return to it; it will never be known again; it vanishes like smoke. Sometimes a lover is so struck by the

death of the old life that he mourns it like any death, perhaps even with wondering tears. This does not mean that
he wants to reenter it, a fact that the beloved may find
hard to understand. When one puts away childish things,
one may mourn the death of childhood, yet one would not
wish to go back to being a child. Anyone so perverse as to
attempt to do so would not only fail to regain the old life,
but lose the new one, too. To pass into romantic love, then,
is to pass from life, through death, to another, different life.
Because I die, I live. I have lost myself; I am beside myself;
I am outside myself. Yet just because I am outside myself,
for the first time I seem to be my real self, unknown and
unknowable till now. Some mysterious string still connects
me with my old self, as threads join me with my ancestors.
But just as my ancestors have passed away, so, almost as
though I were one of them, have I.

Each moment of romantic love has an infernal counterpart, a twin, for evil is a disorder in something that would
otherwise be good. The mode in which the *incipit vita nova*
is corrupted is that the old life doesn't just die; I slay it. I murder it for the sake of a counterfeit new life, which is really
the prolongation of the slaying. The name of the slaying is
unfaithfulness. How often it is committed under the forged
signature of the *incipit vita nova*! I glamorize the betrayal of
love in the name of love itself: "Love made me do it."

Behold a god more powerful than I. Dante said of
Beatrice, "The moment I saw her I say in all truth that
the vital spirit, which dwells in the inmost depths of the
heart, began to tremble so violently that I felt the vibration
alarmingly in all my pulses, even the weakest of them. As it
trembled, it uttered these words: *Ecce deus fortior me, qui
veniens dominabitur mihi,* 'Behold a god more powerful
than I who comes to rule over me.'"[11]

Notice who is speaking: not Dante, but his vital spirit,

his life principle. Notice, too, of whom it speaks: The god more powerful than Dante's life is not Beatrice, but his love for her. The mere process of living acknowledges, in love, a new master; the continuation of life declares itself of small importance. All that until this moment was everything to Dante now moves to the periphery. Everything is seen in new perspective. The lover is no longer his own center, his own circumference, the only being whose good he must consult. There is Another. In this sense, from the dawning of love every lover says *ecce deus fortior me.*

Like the *incipit*, the *ecce* has an infernal double. Dante knows it, for his choice of word, *deus,* can be taken in two ways. We might hold that the immortal God is love, and that mortal love is his image; this thought runs like a golden thread through all of Dante's work. But instead we might hold that mortal love itself is God, and Dante wants us to understand that the temptation to such idolatry is inherent in all love. The soul who is ruled by love sacrifices himself for the true good of the beloved. That is not idolatry. But suppose he goes on to worship her. It he still serving her true good? No, because it is no mortal good to be worshipped; it harms her. But if his worship harms her, then it is no longer loving at all.

We might debate how common it is for someone to worship the beloved herself. But it is not at all unusual for him to worship his own state of adoration—and that is not true love either.

Now your beatitude has been revealed. Dante continues his story[12] with the remark, "At this point, the spirit of the senses[13] which dwells on high in the place to which all our sense perceptions are carried, was filled with amazement and, speaking especially to the spirits of vision, made this pronouncement: *Apparuit iam beatituda vestra*, 'Now your beatitude[14] has been revealed.'"

To Dante, as to every romantic lover, his beloved seems heavenly and flawless. Because all finite beings are flawed, cynics consider this perception a sheer erotic illusion: The beloved couldn't be that wonderful! Is it illusion or not? In the case of mere enchantment, I would say yes, it is an illusion. In true romantic love, however, the matter is more complicated. For the lover is not deceived; his love enables him to see the beloved more clearly than ever, because now he sees her with double vision. With his ordinary eyes Dante sees the everyday girl on the Florentine street well enough—especially her sharp temper. Yet with the other set of eyes, he has a clouded but true vision of the same girl in glory, of her beatific self as distinct from her everyday self—as she would have been in Eden, as she is, potentially, in Paradise.[15]

Dante happens to be extremely intrigued by the power of sight. I use the expression "vision," though, not just for that reason, but also because the experience of which we are speaking does such strange things to the power of sight. To the lover, the beloved may seem luminous, iridescent, as though she were lit up from within, like a paper lantern.[16] Some lovers say that she reflects light from a lamp which is not present; others that she seems to be encrusted with gems. She is almost too wonderful to look at steadily. The experience has the aroma of eternity.[17] When Dante says "Now my beatitude has been revealed," his phrasing is therefore exact. He does not say that the beloved *is* his beatitude; she isn't. Nor does he say that he *possesses* his beatitude; he doesn't. He claims only that because of the vision of her beatific self, the reality and meaning of his own beatitude have been divulged to him. It isn't she who is the infinite and perfect Good. Yet by some magic, by some effulgence of grace, she somehow, to some degree, diffracts or reflects it to him.

In this state, it is perilously easy to make a mistake about the beloved that we mentioned before—to worship her. The idolatry of the beloved is not a form of romantic love, but a perversion of it. So again we meet the infernal twin.

I shall often be impeded. Dante concludes his discussion of his first meeting with Beatrice by explaining, "Whereupon the natural spirit, which dwells where our nourishment is digested, began to weep and, weeping, said: *Heu Miser! quia frequenter impeditus ero deinceps*—'Woe is me! for I shall often be impeded from now on.'"[18]

The lament expressed by Dante's natural spirit is not about his digestion. The bodily location where each principle of action operates is not his point, nor need we accept his biological theory. What he means is that his self-concern was staggered. The woe that is expressed by his natural spirit is not the same as the grief for the death of the old life that I mentioned earlier. It is the stunning shock of the realization that his desires will no longer have their own way. The only true solution to such a predicament is to acquire new desires. The lovers must learn to want goods they are not yet capable of desiring, goods which in their first state they may tremble and weep to conceive.

There is also a false solution. The shock of the fact that from now on our desires will be impeded generates a temptation to reject love itself. In the present age, the fear of being impeded is so strong that we no longer wish to grow up. It is often said that young men and women hesitate to marry these days because now they can have sex without the burden of commitment. This reasoning is too facile, too incomplete. The problem is not that they have found a way to avoid the burden of commitment, but that they have come to view commitment as a burden. What?! Isn't it a burden even in romantic love? Yes, but for lovers, the yoke is light. They want to be burdened, they yearn to be loaded down, they look forward laughingly to the weight. We now pass on to the Shulammitic moments.

A garden locked, a fountain sealed. Though Solomon goes so far as to court the young woman in his personal chambers, she mockingly declares, "My vineyard, my very own, is for myself; you, O Solomon, may have the thousand, and the keepers of the fruit two hundred."[19] The shepherd lover exults, "A garden locked is my sister, my bride, a garden locked, a fountain sealed."[20] Indeed she is for the beloved alone, a garden shut to other lovers, not so that she may wither in a cage, but so that she may offer her secret blossoms behind the protecting walls of a mutual and exclusive gift. The demand that her garden be locked is just as much her demand as her beloved's, and she demands that he lock his garden, too: "Set me as a seal upon your heart, as a seal upon your arm." She gives as her reason that "love is strong as death, jealousy is cruel as the grave."[21]

The declaration that love is strong as death is ambiguous. By itself, it might mean only that there is something in love that cannot die. Surely that is part of the Shulammite's meaning, for she says a moment later, "many waters cannot quench love, neither can floods drown it." Yet between these assuring lines stands a warning, a warning which evokes not endless joy but the danger of final ruin, for love is a jealous god.

I do not mean that love is a narrow, anxious, mean, suspicious, bullying, or unforgiving god, for love cannot willingly withhold any true good from the beloved. That sort of jealousy is but another perversion of love. Yet love gives and demands faithfulness, and it cannot countenance treason or betrayal without becoming other than it is. This then is the "cruelty" of love, that it implacably loathes and inexorably hates whatever is contrary to its own nature, whatever is inimical to life. I say *whatever*, not *whoever*. Relentlessly, it tramples whatever opinions the lovers themselves may have about the matter. Truly it is cruel as the grave, not because it is kin to the grave, but because it is death's sworn enemy, just as implacable as its foe.

Do not gaze at me! There is an element of shyness, of diffidence, in the lover's desire. She wants both to boast and to hide: "I am very dark, but comely, O daughters of Jerusalem, like the tents of Kedar, like the curtains of Solomon. Do not gaze at me, because I am swarthy, because the sun has scorched me."[22] Though she wants to give sweet gifts to the beloved, though she wants to give herself to him, even so she hesitates.

Why does she hesitate? On the one hand she feels ravishing, because she is loved. On the other hand she feels ugly, because she cannot be worthy of so great a thing. A gift immense as love is almost too much to bear. She feels that she should depart, yet she longs to remain, to be as beautiful as he thinks she is, lest she perish of the beauty of his glance. Almost she despairs; the very thought of loving seems presumptuous. It is too greatly daring. She says she is too scorched by the sun to be loved; yet the sun that has scorched her is love itself.

What is her beloved thinking as she makes this speech? We are not told. I imagine that his feelings are complementary to hers. He is soaring like an eagle in her updraft, yet at the same time thinking what a blunt-winged oaf he is, how unworthy of touching her almost-holy flesh with such thick and clumsy fingers.

Though even today such thoughts are not wholly unknown, they are no longer sung. There is much less singing today altogether. We are supposed to think it is the part of the woman to flaunt, the part of the man to grab. Or perhaps, in the name of equality, we make both into flaunters and grabbers. These things do not exalt. It is by modesty that the human heart is most greatly lifted up.

I sought him, but found him not. The lover exclaims, "O that you would kiss me with kisses of your mouth!"[23] What she wants is nothing but him; what she wants to give is nothing but herself. Yet he is absent.

I said before that love has the fragrance of eternity, yet for finite beings it also has a scent of fear, of precariousness, of risk of loss. If it is true that the lovers can bind their wills, yet it is not as though these bonds were made of lifeless substances like iron or stone. They are made of nothing but will. They are made, in a sense, of themselves. Hence the lovers could ruin their love; they could lose it; they could lose each other forever.

There is another element, too. "I opened to my beloved, but my beloved had turned and gone. My soul failed me when he spoke. I sought him, but found him not; I called him, but he gave no answer. The watchmen found me, as they went about in the city; they beat me, they wounded me, they took away my mantle, those watchmen of the walls. I adjure you, O daughters of Jerusalem, if you find my beloved, that you tell him I am sick with love."[24] Yet this sickness of love is something more than the fear that I mentioned a moment ago. What is it, then? Let us reflect that nothing so fully promises completeness as love, nothing so intensifies the longing for completeness by its teasing foretaste of completeness. Yet so great is the yearning aroused by this foretaste that nothing falls so short! Many are those who would rather not love than endure the sickness of love; many who would rather give up that fragrance of eternity, just because it is only a fragrance.

The problem, then, is not that the human lover has withdrawn himself, but that somehow, not even all of him is enough. John of the Cross writes, "Why, after wounding this heart, have you not healed it? And why, after stealing it, have you thus abandoned it, and not carried away the stolen prey?"[25] Both lovers feel this wound. There are two views about it.

According to one view, the lovers desire an impossible degree of union. They want fusion, they want to be really one being. Of course they can't do that. Yet suppose they could. Suppose it were possible for them to merge into a single person, a single mind, a single body, with two heads, four legs, and four arms. Would that perfect their love?

Paradoxically, it would annihilate it, because a necessary condition of the communion of two persons is that they really are distinct persons. Even in conjugal intercourse, when their bodies become "one flesh," the lovers are not a single person, but more like a single organism in which two persons reside. I am not saying that the desire for an annihilating fusion is unknown; I am only saying that it is not love. On one side it is a terrible hunger and appetite, on the other side a wish for death. One of the two persons seeks to absorb and obliterate the other, the other seeks to be absorbed and obliterated. This is not what the Shulammite is speaking of.

The real root of the wound of love that sickens her lies elsewhere. Where, then? I think in the fact that the lovers' desire for each other both ignites, and obscures, a different desire—one they may not have expected and may not even recognize. Their erotic longing provokes a mysterious second longing, of which it, by itself, is only an image. Because this strange second longing is not eros, but is only awakened by eros,[26] it cannot be appeased by eros either. The Shulammite cries to the beloved, "Why, after wounding this heart, have you not healed it?" because he *cannot* do so. This is why she warns those not yet wounded, "I adjure you, O daughters of Jerusalem, by the gazelles or the hinds of the field, that you stir not up nor awaken love until it please."[27]

And yet, O happy chance! she is not sorry for her wound. It is not one that kills, but one that gives life. She would rather suffer the wound without healing, than never have been pierced in the first place; she would rather yearn without fulfillment, than never have been awakened to the yearning.

Sustain me! "Sustain me with raisins, refresh me with apples; for I am sick with love. O that his left hand were under my head, and that his right hand embraced me!"[28] It is easier to understand the cry "Sustain me!" if we consider what it would mean not to be sustained.

Confusion of the two longings, of erotic longing per se with that other longing which erotic longing awakens, brings many lovers to grief. They expect their embraces to satisfy not only the longing that mortal love can satisfy, but also the longing that it awakens, but cannot satisfy. Demanding the satisfaction of the second longing too, they become tyrannical. Discovering that it cannot be satisfied, they misdiagnose the problem. He thinks, *It is the fault of my wife.* She thinks, *It is the fault of my husband.* They think, *It is the fault of our marriage.* Or perhaps they blame faithfulness, promises, or love itself. There is nothing wrong with faithfulness, promises, or love; there may not even be anything wrong with these husbands, wives, or marriages. What vexes these souls is that they are getting the first, appeasable longing mixed up with the second, unappeasable longing.

Suppose we could have the appeasable longing without the unappeasable longing, eros without the divine something that it so terribly resembles. Would that be better? No, for that divine resemblance is the very thing that makes eros what it is for human beings. Without it, eros would only be sex, as it is among the animals—a bodily stress followed by relief, perhaps with an added urge to nest.

And so the lover's cry, "Sustain me!" is a demand not for satisfaction, but for consolation. By means of love, she and the beloved console each other for the inconsolable second desire that their love has awakened. They are, for each other, the balm that makes the sweet wound endurable, even though they are not its remedy. Who knows? Together, they might hunt out whether anything really can appease that second longing. Together, they may find greater success than either could have if they hunted for the answer alone. That is an aspiration truly worthy of love.

Let us bring this little survey to a close. With whatever skill or clumsiness, I have tried to distinguish four things. Enchantment, the first, is the sheer emotional infatuation in which a particular man and woman can't get enough of each other. Charity, the second, is the attitude that exults in the sheer existence of the other person, and which entails a permanent commitment of the will to the other's true good. Erotic charity, the third, is the mode of charity that is particularized toward a single person of the polar, corresponding sex, and consummated by the union of their bodies. Finally, romantic love, in which I have distinguished eight moments, is the mode of erotic charity that enchantment imitates—though enchantment is a matter of the feelings, romantic love a matter of the will.

Enchantment cannot be promised. Even though romantic love is at bottom a matter of the will, when it sings in the romantic key it calls forth such a dense interweaving of passions, desires, and volitions that it cannot be promised either. But charity can be promised, and erotic charity can be promised. It is terribly important that they can, because they are a preparation—so far as anything can prepare—for the strange transcendence that I have promised not yet to discuss.

5

The Meaning
of Sexual Beauty

Reveal your presence,
And let the vision and your beauty kill me,
Behold the malady
Of love is incurable
Except in your presence and before your face.
                    —John of the Cross, *Spiritual Canticle*

D inner would be served in a few minutes. Over glasses of wine, the women were exchanging compliments about their appearance. Cora told Kathryn she looked sexy. Kathryn was pleased. I was much younger than I am now, and something of a boor. Something got into me. I turned to Cora.

"Both of you are lovely—"

"Thank you."

"—but what do you mean when you call Kathryn 'sexy'?"

"I mean attractive. Desirable."

"Forgive me if I'm too literal," I answered, "but what desire do you mean?"

"Sexual desire. What else would I mean?"

"So the basis of your compliment is that the way Kathryn looks makes men want to get in bed with her?"

"Sure."

"All men?"

"Sure."

"That's good?"

Cora and Kathryn glanced at each other and laughed. "Is it strange that a woman would want to be desirable?"

"Well, you wouldn't want to have sex with all men, would you?" I asked.

"No," Kathryn said.

"Then why would you want all men to desire to have sex with you?"

"Don't you understand a woman wanting to be beautiful?" asked Cora.

"Sure," I said.

"Well, then?"

"But you didn't speak of beauty. You spoke of sexiness."

"Aren't they the same thing?" they both exclaimed.

"I don't think so," I replied. "A man can be moved by a woman's beauty without wanting to go to bed with her."

Chris, Cora's husband, broke in. "That's impossible," he said.

Michael, the other husband, suggested, "No, I get it. You're thinking of her attraction as a purely aesthetic quality, completely unrelated to sex. Right? So for you a woman's 'beauty' is like the beauty of a sunset, of an abstract painting, or of a mineral formation."

"Not at all," I answered. "The beauty of a woman affects me in a way that the beauty of a man doesn't. Obviously the experience is sexual, in the sense that it's connected with the difference of sex."

"If it's sexual," agreed the husbands, "then it's all about sex." Their wives thought so, too. Such as it was, the conversation was over.

Well, the young oaf got what was coming to him. As someone more discreet laughingly pointed out to me later, I should have known better than to mix it up at a wine and dinner party. If Socrates and Alcibiades had been there, then maybe yes. Otherwise, no. That was all true.

But the dinner-goers had only delivered opinions; they hadn't solved the puzzle. What is the solution? A normal man, for example, finds it highly interesting to contemplate womanly beauty, and obviously it is all related to the difference of sex. But is it "all about sex"?

How can one explain something that is so obvious to some and so invisible to others?

To a man, women seem to glow in more hues than men do, and in different ones. The spectrum is wider, the world has more music and color, just because there are women in it. Of course there are certain things a normal man rightly prefers to do with other men, like playing tackle football. Yet the very light and air seem to change when a woman leaves the room, and all men know it. Obviously this fact is connected with her bodily presence: with the sound of her voice, the delicacy of her gestures, the way she possesses herself. But it isn't about imagining her naked. The heart of a man who loves classical ballet is affected by the grace of the woman's movements in an entirely different manner than by the strength of the man's, but it isn't about wanting to have sex with her. Any man who is not a barbarian is awed by the self-contained serenity of the figure in Vermeer's "Woman Holding a Balance," and the aura of mystery and inwardness that her image evokes is strongly connected with her being a woman, but it isn't about picturing her in bed. The aureole is destroyed by doing that. (Doubters, no doubt, will verify this fact by experiment.)

And have I mentioned the eerie splendor of antiphonal singing, call and response, in which the men sing the even lines and the women sing the odd? One might think it would be the same thing to have the low voices of both sexes sing the even ones, and the high voices of both sexes sing the odd. It isn't. Antiphony is an altogether different thing, the beauty of the counterpoint of two different and complementary kinds of beauty. One feels, upon listening, as though manhood itself sang to womanhood, and womanhood made reply. It is a musical proof of the natural theorem of the correspondence of the two polaric sexes.

The most telling point in favor of the view that sexual beauty really is all about sex is that if a man contemplates a woman's beauty long and intensely enough, he is pretty likely to begin daydreaming about sex with her (a good reason not to admire her too studiously). Logically, though, how compelling is this point? If the image of her in bed does chase out other thoughts, then plainly they are not the same thought. Would we say that because a student who works on his calculus homework long enough may daydream about doing something fun, this proves that calculus is "all about fun"?

Reproach me not, O Freud, with your incantations; settle back in your grave. The murmur that P is a "sublimation" of Q doesn't prove that P is all about Q. It only assumes that it is.

So many different elements are present in our response to the other sex. I mean both the man's response to the woman and the woman's response to the man, but it would be awkward to keep going back and forth between "he" and "she." Since I am a man, it is more convenient to write about sexual beauty just in terms of female sexual beauty.

This imparts a certain one-sidedness to the chapter, but most of what I say about female sexual beauty has analogies—not parallels—in men. To discuss all these analogies would take several additional chapters. That might be worth doing in another book. Not here.

Consider, then, but a few of all the things men report experiencing in the presence of a lovely woman, not counting the fantasy of receiving her favors:

- The suggestion of another world
- A divination of unseen things
- A sensation of hiddenness
- An increase in liveliness
- The feeling that the air has become fresher
- Delight in what meets eye and ear
- Enjoyment of her differentness
- Pleasure in her conversation
- An occasional and not entirely displeasing exasperation
- Heightening of delight in the other things taking place nearby
- Heightening of delight in other people who are present
- A desire that those people would go away
- A feeling of clumsiness
- A feeling of the clumsiness of the male sex as a whole
- Amusement over the two previous thoughts
- Embarrassment over the two previous thoughts
- Acceleration of the tempo of thought
- Calming of the tempo of thought
- Confusion
- A sense of precariousness

What compels us to try to reduce all these responses to just one response? We laugh at the sages of ancient times who speculated that all of the various things in the universe were made of just a single element, water, yet we admire the alchemists of modern times who speculate that all of the various things that awaken in a man's soul in the presence of a woman are made of just a single element, lust.

I do not wish to be misunderstood. On one hand, the fact that the power to be moved by the beauty of the other sex can change into sexual appetite doesn't show that it is the same thing as sexual appetite. On the other hand, this passive potentiality, this possibility of turning into sexual appetite, is also a real fact.[1] Under the present condition of human nature, it imparts even to innocent admiration a kind of danger. That is one of the reasons for the sense of precariousness that I mentioned above. A wise man governs his eyes, not because it is wrong to delight in beauty, but because otherwise his delight may suffer transmutation into something very different.

But a cool discussion of sexual beauty is difficult. Our opinions are so hot, so extreme. One kind of fanatic wants to compel all women to wear the burqa. Another kind wants to make them all bare their breasts. Fortunately, our perceptions are not always as crass as our opinions. We notice much more than the fashionable manias of the day encourage us to notice. So let us try to disentangle sexual beauty from what Kathryn called sexiness, beginning with the former.

The beauty of a lovely woman has three elements. One element is the beauty of her humanity, of that which makes her a rational being. Another element is the beauty of her femininity or womanliness, of that which makes her a woman. The last is the beauty of her personality, of that which makes her who she is. The first is common, the second polaric, the third particular to herself. Although we can distinguish them, these elements work together. In particular, only a rational being can have beauty of person, because only a rational being is a "who." Each of these three elements may also be developed to greater or lesser degrees. When I speak of a woman's sexual beauty, though, I am referring only to the second element, her womanliness.

In turn, although womanliness is a single thing, I may admire it in two different ways. As a rational being, I may respond, "How wonderful it is in itself, that such creatures exist!" But as a man, I may exclaim, "How wonderful it is for such creatures as me, that such creatures exist!" The first is delight in the beauty of women per se; the second is delight in the difference, the correspondence, the complementarity of their sex to my own.

I explained in chapter three that the essential difference between men and women, the underlying reality that gives rise to all their other differences, is that men are in potentiality to be fathers, and woman in potentiality to be mothers. All those things about a woman that arise from this difference, such as warmth, tender-mindedness, and sensitivity to the emotions of others, are signs of this potentiality. The more fully they are developed, the more intense and beautiful her womanhood, and the deeper its complement to manhood.

We also saw in that chapter that potentiality for motherhood is not about physical possibility but about design, and that motherhood can be not only bodily and directed toward the marital estate, but also spiritual and directed toward another estate. This explains the beauty of someone like Teresa of Calcutta. It is no accident that she was called "Mother" Teresa. Though she set aside the whole business of erotic love, marriage, and physical conception, her beauty was that of a holy woman, distinct from the beauty of a holy man; the qualities that distinguish women from men were distilled, concentrated, and spiritualized in her. This kind of beauty also has its signs, its radiance, and its glory, and it is utterly womanly.

On the other hand, Teresa's kind of womanly beauty was not what we normally call sexy. So what is sexiness? I confess that I dislike the word. It is a harsh word, coarse and brazen. Then again, in our time almost all of the words used for speaking of matters sexual have acquired coarse overtones. So rather than avoiding the word, perhaps we might try to redeem it.

The man on the street would say that a woman is sexy if it would be pleasant to have sex with her, but the matter is not quite so simple. For what does he mean by having sex? He may answer, "engaging in a physical act," but surely he doesn't mean a purely physical act. It is very rare for anyone to seek just the physical act of sex, removed from all semblance of personal relationship. If that were the goal, the woman might just as well be unconscious. Except, perhaps, for those rapists who drug their victims with Rohypnol, the act of sex is almost always to some degree relational—even if the relationship is short, shallow, cruel, malignant, or imaginary. Some sort of conversation takes place even in hookups with strangers. Some fantasy of a real woman takes place even in using pornography. Utterly depersonalized sex, sex without reference to real or fictitious persons, would be something like absolute zero, a theoretical possibility rarely if ever achieved in reality. Animals have sex like that. Humans don't.

On the other hand, there are various degrees of minimally personalized, or partially depersonalized sex. In certain women we find an ensemble of qualities that signify the prospect of having it. Probably, these are the qualities which that man on the street had in mind. But since sexiness in this sense is at odds with what humanizes sex, we shouldn't call it sexiness per se. We should call it dehumanized sexiness.

At the other extreme from dehumanized sex is fully humanized sex, sex in the context that enables it to bear its full personal meaning, as the mutual gift of each self. Viewed from this context, which is faithful marriage, sexiness is a different ensemble of qualities—those that send the message, "This is a nice person to marry, love, and have children with." By contrast with the other kind, we may call this humanized sexiness.

Insofar as humanized sexiness is the outward sign of the underlying reality that I have called sexual beauty, it closes the circle we opened. We began with sexual beauty; starting over with sexiness, we have ended with sexual beauty. The theme has now been stated. The rest is variation.

One can admire sexual beauty from either of two points of view. One of them is outside the game: "Whoever wins her is a lucky man." The other is inside the game: "I'd be a lucky man to have her." I emphasize the difference because when people say, "it's all about sex," part of their meaning is that no man is outside the game. That is merely the excuse of greedy people who cannot admire anything without wanting to have it as their own. Some are like that about money, some about food, and some about sexual beauty. The names of these vices are avarice, gluttony, and lust. Vices are potholes in the landscape of character, but no one is compelled to fall into them. The great thing is to keep an eye on one's feet, and watch where one is going.

Natural sexiness can also be viewed from different positions in time. The signal sent out by an unmarried woman's beauty is prospective. It is couched in the conditional tense: "I *would be* a nice person to marry, love, and have children with." Since the exchange of physical love is a part of that marital mix, the qualities that would make it delightful are certainly a part of the ensemble. Should we be surprised that a certain kind of young man, brought in range of her charm, finds it hard to think of anything else? It doesn't follow that sex is what girl-next-door sexiness "is all about." It isn't about readiness for sex, but readiness to be courted. If the girl is to be successful in finding a loving mate, young men must be able to tell that she would be a loving mate, too.

By contrast, the signal that the beauty of a married woman sends is couched in the present tense: "I *am* a nice person to be married to, love, and have children with." Over the years it ripens to present continuous: "I *have been* a nice person to be married to, love, and have children with." The former sort of signal might seem superfluous. What need has a woman to broadcast her lovability if she is already loved? It might also seem dangerous: Doesn't broadcasting her lovability risk the covetousness of other husbands? Partly for these reasons, a certain kind of Puritanism clamps a lid on the pot, demanding that married women try to repress the signs of lovability. Such efforts miss the point. Rather than protecting marriage, they probably undermine it.

How could they undermine it? One reason is that the sexiness of his wife reminds a husband of his joy in her, and confirms him in his faithfulness. Imagine what a cheat the world would seem if the moment he married her, all women continued to seem beautiful except for her! An even bigger reason is that a sexually beautiful married woman can't entirely turn off her sexiness. It isn't something she contrives, but something that glows from her. Not that women don't contrive it too; of course they do, and we will come back to this. But the most compelling and believable signs of being a nice person to marry, make love with, and have children with are the ones that arise spontaneously. They are an outward glory given off by an inward and invisible reality. A beautiful woman cannot help giving off such radiance, because it is an effect of what she really is.

Although everyone within range of such radiance notices, it is not an invitation to prurience. Think of it as the silent voice of her womanliness. Nature does not intend the same effect on each recipient. "Hearing" her silent voice, her husband rejoices in his happiness with her. "Overhearing" it, their friends rejoice in their happiness. "Resonating" with it, they rejoice in their own happiness. Resonance is common at weddings. As the married friends of the bride and groom witness the grave exchange of vows, they feel as though they were reenacting their own vows. For the moment, husbands are more aware of what draws them to their wives,[2] wives of what draws them to their husbands.

I have been calling sexiness an outward sign of the inward reality of the beauty of womanliness itself. Perhaps this is the time to inquire more deeply into the nature of signs. A sign is something that signifies something else, but not only are there different "something elses," there are different ways of signifying them.

Some signs bring about the things that they signify. These are called efficacious signs. A decree of adoption, for example, is an efficacious sign because it not only signifies the adoption, but actually accomplishes it in law. We are not presently concerned with that kind of sign. The kind that concerns us is the kind *brought about* by what it signifies. For instance, heat, fleeing crowds, and cries of "Fire!" are all brought about by fire, and they signify its activity. They aren't signs because they make fire happen; they are signs because it makes them happen.

Although heat, fleeing crowds, and cries of "Fire!" can all be caused by fire and can all signify fire, they are not cut from the same cloth. Heat is a *natural* sign of fire, because it is in the nature of fire to produce it; fire cannot help but give it off. The fleeing crowd is an *adventitious* sign of fire, because a fire could occur without making people run, for example if it was burning in a deserted place. The cry of "Fire!" is a *communicative* sign of fire, because people are shouting it just so that it will serve as a sign. Assuming that these people aren't deceivers, their cry is just as much an effect of the fire as are the heat and the fleeing crowds. They cry "Fire!" because there is fire. The difference is that in this case the effect is mediated by an intention of imparting a message. Because of the fire, they want to give warning, and just for that reason, they cry, "Fire!" By contrast, nobody intends the heat of the fire and the fleeing of the crowds to signify fire; they just do.

The point of all these distinctions is to help us understand what kind of sign sexiness is. At the most basic level, girl-next-door sexiness and married-woman sexiness are natural signs of sexual beauty, as heat is a natural sign of fire. It is in the nature of sexual beauty to produce them. Contrived sexiness cannot make a woman sexually beautiful, but if she *is* sexually beautiful, then she *will* be sexy. To put the point another way, the qualities that make her sexually beautiful *simply are* those that make her a nice person to marry, make love, and have children with. Since sexiness is nothing but the sign of them, whatever is a sign of them is sexy.

Now for the complications. So far I have focused on the natural signs of sexual beauty, and I have been speaking as though they were its only signs. Like fire, however, sexual beauty has adventitious and communicative signs, too. An adventitious sign of fire is that people flee; an adventitious sign of sexual beauty is that young men approach. A communicative sign of fire is that people cry, "Fire!"; a communicative sign of sexual beauty is that a woman dabs herself with perfume. The most effective communicative signs of sexual beauty are those that lightly emphasize its natural signs. Pretty ways, for example, may draw a young man into conversation, and in conversation he may discover her character. The least effective communicative signs of sexual beauty are those that fake its natural signs or mask their absence. Although these can be highly effective in the short run, it is in the nature of the case that they are eventually found out. It isn't just that the makeup runs, but that the chatter turns catty. The lie is eventually unmasked.

Natural signs differ in effectiveness in some of the same ways that communicative signs do. Pretty looks are suggestive of the grace of womanliness, but a pretty girl who lacks the grace of womanliness seems less and less beautiful over time, because the thing her prettiness indicates turns out not to be there. Conversely, a physically ungainly girl who does have the grace of womanliness comes to seem more beautiful over time. We laugh when a young man says about a girl that he likes, "She's prettier than I thought." That chuckle may be cynical or appreciative. The cynical view is that beauty is in the eye of the beholder, so if he thinks she is prettier than he used to, it is only because he likes her now. But this cynical analysis is false. Womanly beauty is an entirely real thing, not just in the eye of the beholder but in the woman herself. In fact, the young man's remark about the girl, "She's prettier than I thought," may be more precise than we think. At first, perhaps, he sought only the more obvious delights of endowment, the fullness of lip and the glide of the hip, and found them wanting. But as he has come to know the girl, he has come to discover the subtler charms of her face and form, the ones more expressive of her character: the honesty of her glance, the purity of her smile, the self-possessed grace of her carriage.

Just now I called the subtler charms a discovery. For many people, especially for the young, and especially for young men, it is a difficult discovery to make. The reasons for this fact are not widely understood. We say that young men are more interested than young women in how the other sex looks; that is true, but there is a good deal more to it. The more important difference is that young men tend to be *less* observant than young women of the more elusive aspects of appearance. Consequently, the biggest disadvantage of the plain girl with character isn't that no young man could ever think her beautiful, but that she finds it difficult to get young men to notice her long enough to see just how beautiful she is.

For this reason, I don't agree with those strict people who would deny a woman a pretty dress or a touch of powder on grounds that adornment is an artifice. Artifice need not be dishonest. We don't call it deceitful for a baker to adorn pastry with frosting, or for a speaker to adorn lectures with jests—so long as the pastry and the lecture are really good. Neither should we call it deceptive for a woman to hang a modest pearl from her ear. If the ornament helps to hold a young man's attention long enough for him to notice her ornaments of character, it has served truth very well.

Dehumanized sexiness is a sign of readiness for sex, but not every sign of readiness for sex is dehumanized. Consider a woman at home with her husband. That her voice deepens and her cheeks flush is a natural sign of readiness for sex. That she sets down her book and disappears into another room to freshen up may be an adventitious sign. That she coyly lifts her eyebrow or lingers over a good-night kiss may be a communicative sign. But these signs are fully humanized. They are part of the sharing of their lives.

Ideally, then, sexiness as a sign of readiness for sex is transmitted in the nuptial context. The husband and wife desire the union of their lives, the union of their bodies, and the opening for new life that this union opens up. All these are threads in a single tapestry of married love. Can these threads be pulled apart? We know that they can, but it tears the fabric.

A young man I know says he prefers his girlfriends to be "a little bit trashy." He is interested in women not as possible partners in his life, but as tools for the slaking of his appetites. For any man in this state of character, the visible signs of a woman's sheer willingness to be used will be very arousing. He finds the tool aptitude sexy. Now in itself, the willingness to be a tool is repulsive, because human beings are persons, not things, beings of such a nature that they must not be tools, and whatever disfigures our nature taints our beauty. So we cannot say that the woman seems sexy to him *because* of her sexual beauty. What, then? Should we say she seems sexy to him *despite* her lack of it? That misses the point. She seems sexy to him *just because* of her lack of it. The very qualities that signify her willingness to be a tool, and therefore make her repulsive, also signify her readiness for minimally personalized sex, and therefore attract him. Any personality so damaged as to be willing to be a tool spontaneously advertises her injury; thus, sexiness in this distorted sense is an uncontrived sign of the damage. It is the outward sign of the inner reality of mutilated personality, spoiled honey that attracts wasps instead of bees.

I call it an uncontrived sign of damage; amazingly, some women contrive to heighten it. In a fashion movement of the '90s called "heroin chic," young women chose tints that emulated dead or nearly dead flesh. In a custom less extreme but more widespread today, they expose portions of their undergarments, as though to say, "Look how ready to be a tool I am—I am already undressing." One day in a department store I was surprised by a salesgirl whose slacks were unsnapped, unzipped, and folded open. Because I was trying to look elsewhere, it took a few minutes to realize that they weren't really in process of removal; they were made to look that way. The flaps were held open by stitching. It is hard to believe that a girl would behave in such a way unless there were a surplus of men who were vitiated enough to like it—and perhaps a shortage of young men who weren't.

The erotic feelings of attraction and repulsion were only partly fused in the young man I quoted. After all, he wanted his girlfriends to be only "a little bit trashy," not completely trashy. They had to be defiled enough to be willing tools, but not so depersonalized that they stopped seeming beings with wills. What he didn't reckon on is the fact that this kind of death has a life of its own, for the man and the woman alike. It advances, like gangrene. One may say, "Thus, no farther!" but the line will not hold.

Interestingly, another approach to fashion takes the opposite tack. I mentioned in chapter four that to some lovers, the beloved seems to glow. This kind of luminescence cannot be measured by photometers; the eyes are catching overflow from another kind of light. Even so, some styles of makeup seek to evoke it. These creams and powders pursue more than the shine of healthy skin. They are trying to simulate the aureole that enfolds the beloved as she is seen by her lover. How much better to be truly beloved, so no simulation is needed! Yet who would have the heart to cavil? At least the young woman is imitating something good!

But to come back to earth, what shall we say of Cora and Kathryn, the two wives whose conversation I reported at the start of this chapter?

Cora complimented Kathryn for looking sexy, and Kathryn was pleased. In itself such a compliment might be innocent and charming. It is not the sort of compliment that husbands pay each other, but that is all right; female conversation is conducted by different rules. When Cora was pressed, what she said that she meant was disturbing. Yet perhaps my oafish questions had only placed her in a false position. Perhaps she didn't even quite understand her own meaning.

Older, and I hope not quite such a boor, I would like to think that her compliment to her friend was intended as reticent feminine shorthand for something like this: "Kathryn, how exquisitely womanly you look, how you glow! I can see how luminous your joy is in Michael, and how proud he is to stand so tall at your side. How happy all your friends are to see you. I feel more radiant to see your radiance, more graceful to see your grace, more married to see your marriage."

Perhaps Cora meant nothing of the sort. But it would have been lovely if she did.

6

The Meaning
of Sexual Purity

Quench my troubles,
For no one else can soothe them;
And let my eyes behold You,
For You are their light,
And I will keep them for You alone.
— John of the Cross, *Spiritual Canticle*

had just finished a public lecture about the married state, the single state, and sex. During the question and answer time, a tall young woman raised her hand to say, "If *that's* what marriage really is, you're pushing me away from it more and more."

The ambiguity of her phrasing intrigued me. Was I the force repelling her from marriage, or was the repulsive force "what it really is"? The point I had emphasized about marriage is that the spouses mutually give themselves to each other, and that it is good to be shaken out of the iron cage of selfishness into sacrificial love.

"I take your aversion to marriage seriously," I said, "and I can think of three possible reasons for it. One is that I've presented the subject so badly that I've made something lovely look ugly. Another is that what disgusts you is the beauty of marriage itself—perhaps you don't want to be jolted out of selfishness! The final possibility is that although you aren't repelled from the beauty of marriage, still, the more sharply that beauty comes into focus for you, the more strongly you sense that you are meant for a different kind of beauty. You experience the pull of the beauty that you don't see as a push from the beauty you do.

"My advice to you is to look deeply into yourself to find out which of these three things is going on. If it is the first one, then perhaps I need to change. If it is the second, then perhaps you need to change. If it is the third, then perhaps neither of us needs to change, but you should reconsider your vocation. Have you considered the possibility that you are called not to the beauty of marriage, but to the beauty of lifelong chastity?"

To my surprise, rather than arguing she fell silent and her eyes turned into saucers—whether because my answer seemed too crazy for comment or hit too close to home, I couldn't tell. To my greater surprise (since this particular audience had no traditions of lifelong chastity and probably considered it unnatural), another young woman asked, "What if you think you really might be called to that? How can you make it work?"

It seems that the hunger for the clean brilliance of light is not extinguished after all; it only sleeps. So we discussed the practice of purity, the everyday common sense of what makes it wobbly and shaky, what makes it soaring and strong.

We shouldn't be surprised that sexual purity is so poorly understood. In our day it is hardly known at all. It is like a lovely blue planet orbiting a faraway, undiscovered star. Considering it important is regarded as the first symptom of a dirty mind. Can we clear some of this up?

In the first place, the very expression "sexual purity" is often misinterpreted, as though it meant sex itself were impure, and purity meant purity from that. Not so, for there are two modes of sexual purity—for unmarried persons, continence; for married ones, faithfulness. If sex itself were impure, there couldn't be a married kind of purity. Marriage would be nothing but institutionalized filth, like temple prostitution. On the contrary, the sexual powers are good, but only when exercised by the right person, with the right person, for the right motives, in the right way, and in the right state, which is marriage. Moreover, the two modes of purity are complementary, because wherever dedicated, continent singleness thrives, faithful, fruitful marriage thrives as well. Loose sexuality is the enemy of marriage, but celibacy is its friend and encourager.

There is also a temptation to think of purity as though it were merely negative, a *no* or *not* lacking character of its own. Again, not so. Certainly, continent singles refrain from sexual intercourse, and faithful spouses from adultery. But those who "get it" aren't just not-doing something; they are doing something. By living as they do, they are pursuing goods of beauty and integrity that impurity undermines and sullies. Even today most people have some idea how this claim might be true in the case of marriage. We grasp well enough that faithfulness isn't merely added to married life, as raisins may be added to bread; faithfulness is intrinsic to married life, as flour is intrinsic to bread. What I am suggesting is that exactly the same sort of thing is true of singleness. If we think of continence merely as not-being-married, or not-having-sex, the insight escapes us. Think of it instead as the flour of a different kind of bread. The single estate is another mode of life, capable of its own kind of integrity, an integrity to which continence belongs in the same way that faithfulness belongs to the integrity of marriage.

I concede that purity is easier in the married state than in the single. Our wisdom traditions used to call marriage a "remedy for lust," making a true point that is almost always misconstrued. Lust isn't sexual desire per se, but disorderly sexual desire—the problem isn't the desire, but the disorder. The idea in the old saying about the "remedy for lust" isn't that marriage provides a way to blow off steam when the pressure inside the boiler gets too high, but that the sweet disciplines of married life have a tendency to rearrange our emotions and desires, to help them *become* more orderly. Of course that won't happen if a man does treat his wife as a steam-pressure vent. But part of the meaning of marital purity is that he learns to treat her as a wife.

Has the single life its own "sweet disciplines," other than continence itself, which help make continence easier? We will return to this question. For now let a word suffice: If you are afraid of marriage because you don't think you are ready for that state of life, I would say that perhaps you aren't—but don't think you aren't already in a state of life. You are only in a different one, with its own challenges, in some ways more difficult than marriage. Just as people may succeed or fail at the married state, so they may succeed or fail at the unmarried state. Purity is essential in both.

But *why* is purity essential? Explaining this to adults who haven't lived it is a little like explaining to small children why you can't make friends by bribing or threatening them. They haven't enough experience of friendship. Not all things are easier to understand from inside—for example, suicide and drug addiction aren't—but some things certainly are. Friendship is one of them; it so happens that purity is another. To the philanderer, the sweetness of purity seems faint and hypothetical, though in the actual practice of faithful marriage it becomes more and more glowingly obvious. The same thing happens in deliberately continent singleness. In order to "get it," one just has to practice it. The proof that honey is sweet is the taste of honey. Furthermore, one can't say, "I will take a vacation from impurity just for this evening to see whether purity tastes sweeter." There is no purity "just for this evening." One is pure every evening, or one is not pure. Is it difficult to see, then, why explaining the sweetness of purity to the diligently impure is like explaining the tang of autumn air, or the fragrance of freshly cut apples, to the fish in the sea? I am not blaming the fish. They don't have lungs and nostrils for that sort of thing. We do have lungs and nostrils for purity, even if we aren't using them.

Though I say that the only way to grasp purity is to practice it, one can learn something from refusing it. Though one will never taste the honey, one may certainly come to taste the wormwood. Eventually that bitterness intrudes on the pleasures of sexual intercourse. This dismal fact inspires a certain hope. If only the bitterness becomes great enough, I may finally stop thinking, "next time the wormwood will be sweeter," and instead begin to ask, "why do I keep drinking it?"

Like the taste of purity, the taste of impurity takes time to develop. I think people must be starting this course of lessons much younger than they used to, because disillusionment sets in early. In the first chapter, I mentioned that my students have begun to find it difficult to conceive happiness as a positive quality. They have been let down so often by pleasure that although they may say their lives are indescribably wonderful, they give the lie to this profession by their inability to think of happiness as anything but freedom from pain and disappointment. Weariness of that sort may have two different outcomes. One outcome is what the ancients called acedia, or sloth—a paralysis of the very desire for the sweet and the good, so that the seeker calls off the search; for the rest of his life he lives simply by the habit of his appetites. The other outcome is just the opposite: a quickening of desire for the sweet and the good on the very lip of despair, so the seeker pulls back and seeks more earnestly.

Now and then, if only by a few inches, sheer desperation breaks the heart's lock and cracks open its door. Swiftly darting images of light slip through, although lumbering proofs cannot pass. Once they get inside, sometimes these bright images can push the door open a bit wider, just enough for the proofs to win entrance. For this reason, our wisdom traditions have hinted at the savor of purity not just by argument, but also by painting pictures.

Though I can only sketch them roughly, two such pictures are especially great. Each evokes a different element in the savor of purity. One awakens the feminine intuition of something that must be guarded; the other, the masculine sense of something that must be mastered. Like the two sexes themselves, these two insights are complementary, and neither sex can ignore either one without peril.

First, then, the soul may be pictured as a castle. Around a massive rampart runs a colonnaded portico. Built into the rampart are many and diverse rooms, including armories, sculleries, libraries, wardrobes, and baths. Inside this rampart lies a courtyard; at the center of the courtyard stands the castle; and a quiet garden lies hidden in the castle's secret heart. This garden has a single door, hung with a curtain. At the end of the garden is a throne in which only one may sit, like the Siege Perilous at the round table of Camelot. All manner of folk may make merry in the portico, but the crowd may not tread in the courtyard, lest the castle be invaded and the garden despoiled.

The castle and the garden express a primary intuition for a woman, but a secondary intuition for a man. A man builds a dwelling; a woman is a dwelling. This is true with utmost literalness of the first nine months for every human being, but it is true at many figurative levels, too. Even though a woman speaks more freely of her emotions than a man does, she lives more within herself. She is an emblem of mystery not only to men, but to herself. The very shape of her flesh is a powerful symbol, for the deepest and most secret place in her body, like the deepest and most secret place in her soul, really is open through only a single door, and really is hung with a curtain. When her mother tells her that only one may be enthroned in that Siege Perilous, the knowledge comes to her not as something odd and perplexing, but as the unveiling of a mystery that she dimly sensed already. Now a man's soul also conceals a secret place with a perilous siege, a sanctum that needs to be guarded; it is not for nothing that the English language has traditionally referred to the soul of a person of either sex not as "it" but as "she." Yet his body is made on a different pattern than a woman's, with its life-generative organs outside. It isn't that the idea of a protected place within has no root in him, but he tends to think of the protected place differently, as a citadel or fortress from which to sally out and fight. For him the great question is whether, when he does go forth, he will defend and protect secret places, or trample and vandalize them. The reason for this becomes clearer when we consider the next image.

Second, then, the soul may be pictured as a rider, horse, and lion. I need to describe this image twice, the first time compressed, the second expanded. The rider sits tall in command; the horse swiftly and obediently carries him to his destination; and the lion assists him to overcome his obstacles and foes. Though horse and lion are on good terms not only with the man but with each other, the lion is the nobler of the two beasts, and urges it on in its exertions. This image lacks the bodily resonances of the castle, so it requires a key. The man is not the soul per se, but her power of directive intelligence. Because her intelligence is her highest power, the one through which the "I" most clearly speaks, it is represented not as a beast, but as a man. The horse is the soul's desires; the lion signifies her ardor. Intelligence is in the saddle, because of his calling to be their master.

This time the order of primacy is reversed, for the rider and his beasts express a primary intuition for the man, but a secondary intuition for the woman. Typically, a woman masters herself so that she may protect the secret place inside her; by contrast, the man at first may be scarcely aware that he even has an inside. Not only the pattern of his body, but the whole thrust of his inclinations points him outward. To a much greater extent than a woman, he pushes outside what is in him, and advances upon what is outside him. He is always making things and theories, but when she looks outward, her first thought is other human beings. Even before a man clearly understands what law and royalty mean, it seems obvious to him that unruly things abroad in the world must be brought under royal law. Characteristically, he comes to be aware that his interior contains a sanctum only after he comes to be aware that he has an interior, and he comes to be aware that he has an interior chiefly through the effort to bring his ardor and desire under the royal rule of mind.

If we expand the image of the rider and his two beasts into three different scenes, we get a glimpse of how such royal rule might be accomplished. In each scene, intelligence, desire, and ardor stand in a different relationship.

Scene one unfolds at night. A muddy road stretches out toward the eastern horizon, but the road is hard to see. In this scene the horse is not a horse, but a shaggy-eared ass, and the lion is not a lion, but a scrawny wildcat. In his left hand, the man is holding the ass's reins, though he doesn't seem to know what to do with them; in his right, he is holding a whip. The ass continually brays, "You had better feed me," and whenever it does, the man obeys. All down the roadside he walks in search of things for the ass to eat. Every now and then, he thinks it might be more dignified to ride in the saddle, but whenever he tries to climb into it, the ass rears and plunges to dismount him, then drags him around by the reins. As he is being dragged, the wildcat bites him, yowling, "Do as the ass says!" Sometimes he strikes back at the two animals with his whip. The ass, knowing his mood will pass, sits down on its rump to wait him out. The wildcat cringes, but although it is cowed, it is not tamed. Eyes flaming with anger, it waits its chance to bite again. If anyone asks the man what he is doing, he says, "I'm pursuing my happiness."

In scene two, the man is still there, but the ass has turned into a brawny mule, and the wildcat into a starving leopard. This time the man has some control over his animals, but his command is uncertain because they are more powerful than he is. Although he is seated on the mule's back, trying to direct it down the highway, they are making little progress. Sometimes the mule turns off the road into pasture. At other times it stays on the road and perhaps even gallops, but as often as not, it runs in the wrong direction. Though the man uses whip, reins, and spurs, it detests being checked; twisting its head around to face him, it shows its blocky teeth and brays, "I haven't yet lost my strength. You had better fear me." But then the leopard snarls, punishing the mule by sinking its fangs into its flank. As the mule reverts to sullen obedience, the leopard gives the man dark looks and mutters, "I don't know why I should be helping *you*." The sun has risen, so the man can see the road, but he is ashamed to be seen because he looks so ridiculous. If anyone asks him what he is doing, he says, "I'm trying to be good."

In the final scene, the man is clad in knight's armor, laughing and singing fighting songs. The mule has turned into a white stallion, and the leopard has turned into a great tawny lion. Thunderously purring, the great cat sidles up to the knight's knee and murmurs, "Where is the enemy? Command me!" Snorting and rearing, the stallion neighs, "Where may I carry you? Let me run!" The man guides the stallion with nothing but his knees and a few quiet words. In place of the whip, he carries a sword for making swift work of foes and barriers. Sometimes at a canter, sometimes at a gallop, the three of them head down the high road, straight toward the sun. Although that great orb is so bright that it ought to blind them and so blazing that it ought to consume them, instead it gets into them like molten gold. If anyone asks the man where he is going, he answers, "Toward joy."

As we see played out in these three scenes, desire and ardor are made to be ruled by intelligence, but desire can resist intelligence instead of obeying it. The loyalty of ardor in this contest is uncertain—it may side with intelligence, but it may side with desire, for as we know, a man can become just as angry and ashamed with himself for trying to exert self-control as for not doing so. Even when ardor does side with intelligence, it may do so resentfully, like a slave, rather than loyally, like a servant. For all these reasons, the first efforts of someone attempting purity may seem ridiculous, not only to others but to him. Nonetheless there is something lofty about these efforts, for it is better to try and fail than not to try. Though it may seem at times as though purity were nothing but a mass of difficult rules, the rules themselves are made for a great and beautiful reason, for removal of the obstacles that keep the soul from riding swiftly to the sun and becoming like molten gold.

A word against overstatement. Very few of us in this life seem much like molten gold. Even those who reject the first scene are more like the second than they would wish. Progress down the road is measured not in miles but in inches. Even so, it is measurable. Our efforts become less and less ridiculous; we begin to catch the golden scent of the burning sun even when still far from it. Siegeworks that once would have stopped us, we begin to be able to scale. About those mightier barriers that still exceed our strength, there are rumors of help from the Emperor; but of this I have promised that I will not yet speak.

As the castle is built from many stones, purity is not a simple virtue, but a complex one made up of parts. We cannot pause for each of these component virtues, but three deserve special attention.

One of them is decorum. Today we find it difficult to grasp why decorum should be viewed as something good. We think it means stiff, old-fashioned manners that are based on arbitrary customs and serve no other function but keeping us from relaxing and having a good time. In the Latin language, the original meaning of the term was deeper. Marcus Tullius Cicero, who had much to say about the subject, called attention to the qualities by which we humans stand out from irrational beings. Alone among the animals, we aspire to understand ourselves and the world we live in. In us alone can be found the lofty spirit that gives us courage, by contrast with the sheer angry arousal that makes an animal bold. We alone are attracted to beauty itself, and we alone perceive the beauty of arrangement and order. Most beautiful of all is the arrangement and order of the nature we find in ourselves, for we are the nobility of living things, and ought to be mindful of our high privilege. Such mindfulness does not mean that we must always be grave and may never joke; humor is also a privilege of rationality, for though animals play, they never joke. But even good jokes require measure and proportion. Bearing all this in mind, Cicero defines decorum as the conduct befitting the dignity of man as a rational being. I would add only one point: Decorum is impossible without reverence for that from which man receives his dignity as a rational being; but since that takes me to the threshold of matters I am not yet to write about, again I desist.

The times are so hostile to decorum that conspicuous examples are hard to find. Instead one must use examples of its failure. Even that may be difficult to do. Recently, a colleague and I taught Cicero to a little flock of freshmen. During one session the students were asked for examples of conduct contrary to the dignity of man as a rational being. Normally talkative, they were stymied. How could any behavior be contrary to the dignity of man as a rational being? Isn't "dignity" all relative anyway? When at last they conceded—heads nodding slowly, as though over a difficult point in differential calculus—that perhaps it might not be suitable for the professor to teach with his pants dropped around his ankles, it came as an intellectual breakthrough.

As it turned out, there was no need to invent hypothetical examples. Around the same time, the university sponsored a freshman assembly about choosing a major. Faculty presented pep talks for their fields of study, and student leaders asked them questions. The tone of the event was epitomized by the student-leader question, "If you were a bar of soap, whose shower would you want to be in?" Grinningly, the faculty moderator pressed the faculty panelists to answer. I am sorry to report that they did.

Another element of purity, modesty, is equally mis-understood. We might say that as decorum expresses respect for the dignity of man as a rational being, modesty expresses respect for the fragility of this dignity. In respect for this fragility, one avoids provoking appetites that people should be trying to moderate. Though modesty too is unfashionable, it has a slightly less unfavorable reputation than decorum. Even today, not many people would boast of immodesty; instead they pretend they are being mod-est. The most common form of pretense is that so long as the intention is clean, the act itself is modest. There are two problems with this move. One is that since intentions cannot be seen, immodesty becomes impossible to identify. The other, deeper problem is that modesty concerns more than intentions.

Suppose that one fine summer day, a young woman decides to enjoy the blessings of the sun, so she takes off her clothing, strolls downtown, and promenades as naked as the day she was born. Suppose further that however unlikely it may seem, she isn't trying to provoke, arouse, or get attention. When some men ogle, she coolly thinks, "What lechers they are! But that is not my problem." If other men turn away their eyes, she thinks, "Such prudes! To the pure aren't all things pure?" Even if her intentions are pure, her conduct isn't. Why? Because she has no respect for the efforts of others toward purity. Whether or not she intends to provoke, she provokes; whether or not she intends to arouse, she arouses; whether or not she intends to get attention, she gets it.

Now suppose that a man on the street drapes his coat around the young woman's shoulders and says, "My dear, you need to be covered." Let us say that his objection arises from concern, not for her moral good, but for his own. He is willing to believe that her motives for putting herself on display are entirely chaste; he might even be right about that, because some women do seem oblivious of the precise nature of their effect on men (it is difficult to say just how few). Some would call the poor fellow lecherous. Not only would this be uncharitable, it would also miss the point. He wants her to dress modestly because he doesn't want to be a lecher; he is trying his best to keep order among his feelings and desires, and he wishes that someone would have a care. The young woman is like someone lighting up a cigarette around gasoline. It doesn't matter that she isn't trying to set the gasoline on fire; she ought to be trying not to.

Truly modest folk, then, are not just clean-minded; they also avoid needless provocation to those who are easily provoked. The point is charmingly made by a conversation between two characters in one of the thousand classics we no longer read, Bunyan's allegory *The Pilgrim's Progress*, published in 1678. (It may be helpful to explain at the outset that the name of the first character means not "mentally deficient" but "faint of heart.")

> Now Mr. Feeble-mind, when they were going out of the door, made as if he intended to linger. The which, when Mr. Great-heart espied, he said, "Come, Mr. Feeble-mind, pray, do you go along with us. . . . [Y]ou shall fare as the rest."
>
> *Feeble-mind.* "Alas, I [lack] a suitable companion. You are all lusty[1] and strong, but I, as you see, am weak. I choose, therefore, rather to come behind, lest, by reason of my many infirmities, I should be both a burden to myself and to you. I . . . shall be offended and made weak at that which others

can bear. . . . Nay, I am so weak a man as to be offended with that which others have a liberty to do. . . . It is with me, as it is with a weak man among the strong, or as with a sick man among the healthy. . . . So that I know not what to do."

Great-heart. "But, brother. . . . [y]ou must needs go along with us. We will wait for you, we will lend you our help, we will deny ourselves some things . . . for your sake. . . . We will be made all things to you rather than you shall be left behind."[2]

Today this sweet passage provokes laughter. It shouldn't. One of its endearing points is that courtesy cuts both ways: Mr. Feeble-mind endeavors to bear with those who enjoy conduct which he knows to be innocent in itself, but which his feelings cannot bear; Great-heart endeavors to bear with Feeble-mind's weakness, denying himself some of these things just so Feeble-mind will not be left alone. We see here the unity and mutual dependence of great virtues like purity, modesty, charity, kindness, and forbearance. How great the contrast between the modesty of travelers on Bunyan's high road, and the immodesty of travelers on ours, a boulevard on which every brassiere is exposed, every pair of boxers is divulged, and every sort of cleavage lifts up its glad face to the sun. Yet there is a lighter side. One fine evening in my neighborhood, I noticed a fellow escorting his young lady across the street. So gently he guided her by the elbow. It would have seemed gallant, if his other hand had not been occupied in holding up his pants.

It is sometimes said that modesty is sexy. When people make this suggestion, they usually mean something crude: that if you want to arouse, you will succeed even better by cultivating the suggestion of something hidden. Movies, for example, are thought to have been more sexually electrifying back in the days when the Hays Code was enforced, so that all that sort of action had to take place off-stage. But however crude the intention of the saying, it also conceals a germ of chaste truth. One's most precious treasures, he hides; no one piles his diamonds on the street. Modesty suggests that there is something of great beauty and worth to be concealed; immodesty suggests that it is too plain and cheap to need concealment. In the final analysis, lust extinguishes more fires than it starts; the ardent flame of love can burn only when shielded from that wind.

We have room to mention just one more brick in the ramparts of purity. I mean temperance. Temperance expresses a certain quality that all virtue has, but expresses it more strongly: the need for order and measure, the need to find the mean, the point of balance, for the danger of ruin may lie in both excess and deficiency. I don't wish to be viewed as claiming that every kind of conduct has a mean. As the noble Aristotle pointed out, it would be absurd to say that the good man commits adultery with just the right woman, at just the right time, and in just the right way, for he doesn't commit it at all.[3] Yet although there is no mean of adultery, there is a mean of certain things related to adultery. It is good that Bruce doesn't sleep with his next-door neighbor's wife, but it is ridiculous if he is afraid to greet her as he is picking up his newspaper, for fear that he may go on to sleep with her. The mean lies not between sleeping with her too much and not sleeping with her at all, but between excessive familiarity and neurotic discourtesy.

Finding the mean requires judgment. What if Bruce merely chats with her? Probably fine (although if she is the neighborhood seductress, maybe not). What if he merely flirts with her? That case is different, because flirting isn't mere. It implies a possibility, plays with it, and invites the other party to play with it, too. To vary the example, it is good that young Felix doesn't sleep with his girlfriend Felicia, but it is probably silly to be afraid of a touch of lips upon parting.

Then again, a touch that feels like a light summer breeze to David and Doris may hit Felix and Felicia like the blast of an open furnace. To put it a bit crudely, a good test is this: Would that touch get my motors running? An evening of recreational kissing on the sofa would fail the test, because revving up the motors is its whole point. Whether a good-night kiss starts the motors is an empirical question, because some motors start more easily than others. One must learn one's own vulnerabilities, as assiduously as seducers study the weak spots of their prey.

Another test is whether what I am doing produces misleading feelings or expectations. Interestingly, this isn't just about social signals. Such is the chemistry of the brain that the longer a good-night hug lasts, the more it produces the feeling of a bond, even if one is thinking "this doesn't mean a thing." The lesson would seem to be that unless you are already attached, it would be a good idea to keep those hugs short. Don't blame me. Blame oxytocin.

I can imagine protests. "Why didn't anyone *tell* me that it only takes ten seconds or so for my brain to release oxytocin? Why didn't anyone *tell* me that my vulnerability might be even greater in the dark?"

These are the wrong questions, for such little findings of brain science merely ratify common sense. Long before people knew about neurotransmitters, they understood that it was wise not to stay out too late, smart not to turn out the lights, and good to put limits on the touching of bodies. Long before they knew that the frontal lobes aren't fully developed until about age twenty-five, they knew that young people need supervision and shouldn't be left alone. Long before they knew how the endocrine system works, they knew that exhaustion and inactivity make not only the muscles but the virtues lose their tone, so that if one doesn't want the mice of temptation to turn into ravening beasts, one must get proper sleep and exercise. Once upon a time, such bits of mother wit, gleaned from centuries of experience, were passed on from generation to generation. To us they seem new because we have broken the generational transmission belt and forgotten what everyone used to know. Instead of turning to our grandmothers, we turn to biochemists. We believe the obvious only when we can isolate it in a test tube.

There is another reason why common sense about purity is so difficult to preserve: Every slip from purity seems self-validating. Sex doesn't just feel good; it feels right!

But every passion and appetite is like that. When food is delicious, eating feels right; when someone has wronged me, slugging him feels right; when someone is a fool, mocking him feels right. We are designed to feel that way, and it makes sense for us to be, for in each of these cases, something generically good is really accomplished. Whenever I eat, I achieve the good of nutrition; whenever I slug someone who has wronged me, I achieve the good of requital; whenever I mock a fool, I achieve the good of calling attention to the truth. So of course these things feel right! The problem is that although they are generically good, it doesn't follow that they are actually good for me, in this way, or in this case. I may be obese and have no need of more nutrition; slugging the wrongdoer is a notoriously untrustworthy pathway to justice; mockery doesn't usually make fools wise, and it almost always lacks charity. In the same way, something generically good is also accomplished whenever we have sexual intercourse. We do achieve one-flesh union, we do open a possibility of new life. So of course it feels right! It doesn't follow that the act is actually good for me, at this time, or with this person.

Needless to say, the passions and appetites cannot make such distinctions for themselves; they need the royal rule of wisdom. Again I imagine protests. "How can I be blamed, when I'm only doing what comes naturally!"

The answer is that for humans, blindly following passion and desire *isn't* what comes naturally. The lower animals are ruled in that manner, but our nature is higher. What most fully develops and humanizes us is for desire and ardor to submit to the rule of wisdom. It isn't even truly possible for us to live "like animals." Even if we seek meaning by taking up the ideology that we are just like irrational beasts, we aren't really like irrational beasts, because for them, it isn't an ideology. They aren't seeking meaning; they don't need it. They aren't taking up anything; they are just doing something. Intelligence transmutes everything. It imbues all passion and all desire with significance unknown to the animals. So the very attempt to be like animals fails inevitably. We use our directive intelligence whether we want to or not, and may as well learn to use it well. Living "like animals" isn't really living like animals, but only living badly as humans.

Earlier in the chapter, commenting on the sweet disciplines of married life, I asked whether the single life has sweet disciplines of its own, disciplines which may help to make continence easier. The answer is "Yes," and we are now in a position to spell it out.

There is the sweet discipline of contemplating the feminine intuition of a secret that must be guarded.

There is the sweet discipline of meditating upon the masculine sense of a strength that must be mastered.

There are the sweet disciplines of decorum, modesty, and temperance.

There are the sweet disciplines of all those bits of mother wit that the old used to pass on to the young.

There is the sweet discipline of governing the gates of the eyes and ears.

I have already touched on the fact that a man's and woman's motives for practicing these disciplines will probably be somewhat different. She, more conscious of the secret place within, guards her purity because she loves it for itself. If he loves purity, he probably arrives at it by a more roundabout route. Whereas the woman guards purity, the man characteristically sees himself as guarding, not purity, but her. But how can she truly guard purity without teaching it to him? And how can he truly be her guardian unless he learns to love her loves? For him, it is not a matter of self-consciousness to honor purity, but a matter of strength: the strength of a protector, the strength of a master of himself.

Once again, by the way, we see that the chivalric ideal is not a quaint medieval invention, but something that grows from deep roots in the soil of a man's nature. Something like the chivalric motive may well be psychologically necessary for a male to learn why chastity is noble. In so many stories, the hero must suffer a test or trial, not only to prove himself worthy of the beloved, but to become worthy of her. For men, chastity is such a trial. Here lie the rudiments of a third great image to be laid alongside the images of the castle and the knight: the image of a scrutiny or ordeal. But as the writers of mathematics books say, this theorem is left as an exercise for the reader.

In a fallen world, no such ideal, chivalric or not, can guarantee its results. When we teach men to perfect their masculinity through the discipline of chivalry, two kinds of men result. The most masculine and spirited will accept the discipline and become knights, but the least masculine and spirited will refuse the discipline and become cads. Impatient with such failures, our age pursues a different ideal. Instead of encouraging men to become knights, it discourages them from being men at all. But this works no better; in fact, it works worse. Again two kinds of men result, but the pattern is different. The most masculine and spirited reject the discipline and become cads, and the least masculine and spirited accept it and become poltroons.

By nature, women prefer lofty manhood to corrupt manhood. But by nature, they prefer even corrupt manhood to what is hardly male at all. Given a choice between knights and cads, and allowed to choose freely without coercion or ideological pressure, most will choose knights. But given only a choice between cads and poltroons, most will choose cads. That is the reason for the paradoxical attraction of so many contemporary young women to "bad boys." If males who seem like girls with pants on hold no interest for them, can you blame them? They prefer the male's edginess. There is no point in telling them, "Don't be attracted to that edge," for the edge is what makes men male.

The problem isn't that men have an edge, but that in a nonchivalric culture, the edge is ragged. It has to be honed, polished, and oiled, like any noble blade. Everything depends on how skillfully the whetstone is applied. Well whetted, the result is confidence; poorly whetted, the result is just attitude. Well whetted, courage; poorly whetted, just stubbornness. Well whetted, ardor; poorly whetted, just moodiness. One kind of man is on fire to protect those who need him; the other is smoldering to exploit them.

Young women also bear part of the blame. So often, seeing the choices they make, they are frightened. The problem isn't that they choose men with an edge, but that they choose men who are rusty pocketknives when they could hold out for diamond-edged swords. Though men place too little worth on protecting them, women place too little worth on that which needs protection. As men allow themselves to be emasculated, women allow themselves to be defeminized. Defeminization even becomes a point of pride and flattery. Authors who write for young females call them "grrls" and tell them not to languish in towers, looking for knights on white stallions. I don't know what they mean by languishing in towers, but I do know this: If you are looking for a man, but you run away from knights, you'll end up running after punks.

It might be held that I have gotten everything backwards. The way I tell the story, the woman is the natural guardian of purity. She teaches it to the man, who, as her natural protector, learns to love purity, too. Denying this, some say the man, not the woman, is the natural guardian of purity—but that he is the guardian of hers only. As they tell the tale, her purity is the only way he can be sure that the children she bears are his own. She learns purity because it is the only way to hold him. He lacks a motive to learn it.

The question, then, is what interest a man could possibly take, not in her purity, but in his own.

I might say to a skeptic that purity protects the very center of a person from invasion by desires that try to master him, rather than being mastered by him. Presumably, though, we are speaking of the kind of man who cannot grasp the point about invasion—who either lives so much on the outside of himself that he does not know he has an inside, or who knows that he does, but thinks his desires are all there is to it. Can anything further be said to him?

Even if he cannot grasp the point about invasion, still he might grasp the point about mastery. So I might point out to him that temperance is a virtue even in the pagan scheme of things. If a man is not to court utter ruin, he must exercise self-control about passions, pleasures, and desires. But wouldn't this sort of man still complain? Perhaps he would say, "I take your point about temperance, but isn't it the same as moderation? Doesn't it lie in avoiding both extremes? Why then must one abstain from *all* sex outside of the little stricture you call marriage? Why should the mean between 'too much' and 'too little' be 'not at all'?"

"Let us think of it your way," I might answer. "At least you admit that the purity of the woman is the only way a man can be sure he is the father of her children. But can't you see that the purity of the man is the only way a woman can be sure that her children will know their father? The fact that you want assurance that your children are your own proves that you have an interest in your children. Then why don't you follow through? All these goods—the integrity of marriage, the integrity of family, the well-being of the children, and the purity of both men and women— depend on each other."

Yet again the protester may object: "That may give good reason for the married to be faithful, but you haven't given reason for bachelors to be continent. Think of the children, you say. Haven't you heard of the pill?"

I might tell him, "Not only have I heard of the pill, I have heard the old predictions that it would put an end to out-of-wedlock pregnancy. Did it? That bomb set off such a landslide in sexual attitudes that there are more out-of-wedlock births today than ever before. Children are worse off, women are worse off, and men are worse off. What now? Should we seek even more radical ways to sever sex from the meaning of sex? Haven't we denatured ourselves enough already?"

Anyone who has spoken with this sort of person knows that anything can be denied. He can deny that a sun is in the sky, deny that cold water slakes thirst, deny that a lapful of burning coals will scorch him. If enough people slip below the waves of denial, then eventually the issue will be settled in a different way, not by argument but by extinction. Look across the water. Civilizations dominated by the point of view I have been disputing stop having children; they lose their desire for both physical and spiritual posterity. In this respect, the natural laws, which are also laws of hope, are weirdly self-enforcing, for such people have no hope. They don't notice it leaving, and they don't feel its loss. Hope is not the sort of thing that interests them.

I have not said there is no hope. It isn't their hope, but there is hope. Hope is an inexhaustible river, flowing with cold water, laughing in spate, rushing more rapidly than anyone can run. Anyone who is thirsty may drink.

7

Transcendence

Oh! who can heal me?
Give me at once Yourself,
Send me no more
A messenger
Who cannot tell me what I wish.

—John of the Cross, *Spiritual Canticle*

"Let him kiss me with the kiss of his mouth," she said.
Now who is this "she"? The bride. But why bride?
Because she is the soul thirsting for God. In order
to clarify for you the characteristics of the bride, I
shall deal briefly with the diverse affective relation-
ships between persons. Fear motivates a slave's atti-
tude to his master, gain that of wage-earner to his
employer, the learner is attentive to his teacher, the
son is respectful to his father. But the one who asks for
a kiss, she is a lover.

—Bernard of Clairvaux, *On the Song of Songs*[1]

Before I broach my swift final theme, allow me, even more briefly, to recapitulate the territory that I have covered so far.

The opening of the book was a fugue on two remarks by a student in one of my classes. Harris wanted to believe that sex "doesn't always have to mean something." Yet he found the people of Aldous Huxley's *Brave New World* disgusting, because they made babies in factories, without parents. Though Harris seemed unaware of the conflict, his two reactions were inconsistent. If sex doesn't always have to mean something, then it has no intrinsic meaning. Whatever transient meanings it has for us are like clothing that we drape over it and take off at our whim. In that case, Harris shouldn't have been disgusted. His repulsion suggests an intuition that babies have a right to be conceived in the loving embrace of their parents. But if this is true, then sex does have intrinsic meaning. It signifies the love of the parents and their partnership in new life.

The second chapter approached the idea of the meaning and purpose of sex from another direction. This time the starting point was not Huxley's fictional dystopia, but our own real dystopia, a tangled skein of dismay and discontent that the weavers of the sexual revolution did not foresee. The root of the present sexual unhappiness is not that we have become disillusioned, that we are no longer able to immerse ourselves in the happy dream that something without meaning has a meaning—but that we have become *illusioned*, that we seek happiness in the miserable dream that something with a meaning is meaningless. If only we really could be disillusioned! If only we could regain the savor of reality! The rest of the chapter reaffirmed the intuition of the dual meaning and purpose of the sexual powers, procreative and unitive, but now they were seen to be rooted in natural law, in the principles of the human design. In the end we discovered that so-called traditional sexual morality makes sense after all.

One of the reasons we find sex so hard to understand is that we don't understand the two sexes. As I argued in the third chapter, sanity begins with the fact that men are potentially fathers, and women potentially mothers. This is not just a fact about what kind of thing they might or might not do some day, but about what kind of being they are inwardly aimed at becoming. Our objections to sanity lie mostly in our resistance to four large truths, which I called the duality of nature, the duality of path, body and soul unity, and polaric complementarity. Missing the first mark makes it impossible for men and women to honor each other for what they really are. Missing the second inclines them to view themselves as either male and female beasts or sexless angels. Missing the third makes their bodily differences seem either irrelevant or all-important. Missing the fourth undermines their union and destroys their solidarity as human beings.

Our folkways are torn between two pictures of love. One calls it flighty, unstable, and prone to reversal; the other insists that it bears all things, endures all things, and never ends. If the argument of chapter four is right, then these are not different views of the same thing, but views of different things. Love, to use the term correctly, is an attitude of the will, something that can be chosen, pledged, and promised. It is an erotic mode of charity, particular-ized toward a single person of the polar, complementary sex, and consummated by the union of their bodies. Much of the confusion about it arises from the fact that in its romantic mode, it has an imitator, which has all the attri-butes of love except its essence; this imitator is purely a state of the emotions, without any necessary connection with the will. The rest of the confusion arises from the fact that at least in its romantic mode, sexual love arouses not just one longing, but two, and only one of these can be satisfied by the union of the lovers.

Beauty is even more bitterly misunderstood than love. The beauty of a woman for a man is obviously sexual, in the sense that it is connected with the difference of sex. But is it "all about sex," nothing but an advertisement for intercourse? According to the fifth chapter, no. Yet the idea of an advertisement is not wholly false. A certain ensemble of qualities does send the message, "Here lies the prospect of minimally personalized sex." This name of the message is sexiness in the dehumanized sense, and the underlying reality that it reflects is damaged personality. A different ensemble of qualities sends the message, "This is a nice person to marry, love, and have children with." This message might be called fully humanized sexiness, and the underlying reality that it declares is sexual beauty. But as the previous chapter had explained, motherhood can be celibate and spiritual as well as bodily and marital. So, then, can the beauty of a woman.

Next in the ladder of misunderstandings is sexual purity. Our popular culture can scarcely distinguish it from neurotic hatred of sexuality, and views it as an inverted kind of prurience. I argued in chapter six that actually, purity reflects a healthy respect for the power and meaning of sex. It is not merely not doing something; it is doing something, living a certain way. The two modes of purity are continence, which is intrinsic to the integrity of the single mode of life, and faithfulness, which is intrinsic to the integrity of the married mode of life. A difficulty is that to anyone who does not live purely, its sweetness seems faint and hypothetical, though in the actual practice of faithful marriage or continent singleness it becomes more and more obvious. In order to impart some idea of what this great good is about, I presented and discussed two great images. The image of the castle and garden evokes the characteristically feminine intuition—more difficult, though equally necessary, for men—of a secret that must be guarded. The image of the rider, horse, and lion evokes the characteristically masculine intuition—more difficult, though equally necessary, for women—of a strength that must be mastered. Certain sweet disciplines make sexual purity easier, and certain grave consequences result from its neglect.

My quick wrap-up completed, I can no longer delay the book's final theme.

Yet it is a touchy one.

The touchiness of certain topics always catches me by surprise. Even the topic of happiness can make people cross. One day in a graduate seminar, a student argued vigorously that the sole meaning of happiness is pleasure. There was an edge to her voice.

"Don't you think happiness must be more than pleasure?" I asked.

"Why?"

"Because no matter how much pleasure one enjoys, it always leaves something to be desired."

"There isn't any such thing as *perfect* happiness," she said with annoyance, "just more and less."

"But don't we grade things 'more' and 'less' in relation to a standard?" I asked. She agreed that we do. "But the standard for 'more' and 'less' happiness is complete fulfillment," I continued, "so if there weren't such a thing, not even in principle, then there couldn't be degrees of it either."

"But there *are* degrees of it," she protested.

"Then in principle, there *must* be such a thing as perfect happiness," I answered. "Even if we don't have it. Even if we don't know what it is."

Bitterly, she exclaimed, "The reason we don't know what it is is that there's no such thing. The fact that we always want more is just the way things are. If we're disappointed, we just have to get over it."

I am reminded of a passage in which Thomas Aquinas wrote, "It is impossible for any created good to constitute man's happiness. For happiness is the perfect good, which lulls the appetite altogether; else it would not be the last end, if something yet remained to be desired."[2] It is as though my student had read the passage, but drawn the wrong conclusion. She was determined to pitch her tent on a plain of salt. *I will not be burned. I will not be moved. I will not be taken in.*

But there is an even touchier Unknown than the Unknown Happiness. At the outset of the book, I pledged not to wade into a discussion of that even touchier Unknown until the end, and I have kept my vow. I didn't pledge never to allude to it, because that sort of promise could never have been kept. Threads of allusion are woven through every chapter. Pulling them out would have twisted the book into knots. Yet I have refrained from using these threads for embroidery. May I recapitulate these, too? But perhaps I need not ask. Now that we have come so far, it would be devious not to confess them.

In chapter two, though I wrote about the human design, only once did I allude to the Designer. In chapter three, though I wrote about the masculine and feminine callings, I did not say who called them, and though I quoted the words, "let it be unto me according to your word," I identified neither the speaker nor to whom she was speaking. In chapter four, though I suggested that the desire of the lovers for each other both ignites and obscures another desire that eros cannot quench, I did not say what this second longing is. Though in chapter five, I described certain persons as holy, I declined to elaborate on the quality of holiness itself. Though in chapter six, I spoke of the Siege Perilous at the center of the soul in which only One may sit, I did not say who may sit there. Though my remark that humans are the nobility of the animals plainly implied a distinction between higher and lower beings, which might in turn be taken to imply a highest being, I allowed the implication to lie fallow. Although the chapter closed with an allusion to the virtue of hope, which has both a mundane and a trans-mundane sense, I declined to resolve the ambiguity.

And what about all those quotations from John of the Cross at the head of every chapter? Those who know the poet may have thought I was confused, because he wasn't explaining mortal love; he was using it to point to something higher. Allow me to observe, in my defense, that an image of mortal love can't point beyond itself unless it is faithful at its own level first. Besides, I am making amends. For these last few pages, I will take the image as John of the Cross intended it.

This, then, is the point at which readers who find transcendence offensive may stop reading. I hope, of course, that they won't, lest they miss the point of all the rest.

Nature points beyond herself. She has a face, and it looks up. One may decline to call attention to her uptilted glance. One may put off discussing it. Out of respect for the sensitivities of readers, one may even assure them that they don't have to notice it. Who am I to lay down the law? But there are some things we cannot help noticing eventually, if we bother to see things at all.

What I am trying, so clumsily, to say is that ultimately, human love makes sense only in the light of divine love. The point is not that divine love means something and that human love doesn't. Human love means so much, because divine love means still more.

Doesn't anyone who thinks seriously about our sexual nature know that it longs for completion? Yet anyone who thinks deeply about it also knows that it cannot quite give what it demands. As an inhabitant of heaven has been said to remark, "Human beings can't make one another really happy for long."[3] In a few paragraphs I will qualify that statement. Even so, taken just as it is written, it is true. This is a fact that even the most devoted lovers eventually confront.

But why must it be true? Surely human sexual love is good, and surely it is ordained for our happiness. What could be the problem? Say "problems," for there are two of them.

The first problem may be called the *imperfection* of human sexual love—the fact that we simply do not love well enough. Through all the generations of human history, lovers have been on poor terms with the imperishable Source of love. Imagine a magnet and three iron rings.[4] The magnet is in contact with the first iron ring, the first iron ring is in contact with the second, and the second is in contact with the third. The magnet stands for God, and the three iron rings for our intellect, ardor, and desire. If the first ring pulls away from the magnet, then it cannot keep the other two rings aligned, and they fall, too. In just the same way, if the mind pulls away from the divine lover, then it cannot make ardor and appetite obey it, and they too become insubordinate. Of course some residual magnetism may remain in the rings, but over time it fades, becoming less and less able to link them together. Hence, divided from God, we are divided from ourselves. We don't do what we want; we do what we don't want; we turn traitor to the longings of our hearts. We demand happiness on terms that make happiness impossible. One of the consequences of this division in the self is that we are also split off from our other selves. Men become alienated from women, women from men.

How often are even lovers tempted to use, devour, or take advantage of each other instead of giving themselves to each other! And though I have written "even lovers," couldn't I have written "especially lovers"? Abundance of passion is no remedy for the problem. When the rings pull away from the magnet, the ardor of sacrifice itself is transmuted into selfishness. Seeing this, suffering this, how many mortals give up on love completely! How many others, though giving in to the longing for some kind of love, set their sights as low as possible! At times it may seem that the communion of two beings does nothing but open new possibilities for them to cause each other sorrow. Ah, my dear, if I didn't love you, you couldn't hurt me as much as you do. If you didn't love me, the wounds I give your heart wouldn't sting so dreadfully like death.

What then? Perhaps we become cynics. We read a book like this, or a better one, and we think it is building castles in the air. Or perhaps our disillusionment takes another form, as it did among the Stoics, who were in many ways the greatest of the pagans, yet tragically flawed. They gave up on the seemingly unattainable virtues of the happy life, instead recommending the "middle virtues," which anyone could attain, but which made nobody happy.

I said passion is no remedy, but I did not say that there is no remedy. One must submit unconditionally to the surgery of the divine physician. So great is His compassion that He, who alone is whole and unbroken, inconceivably took our brokenness upon Himself to make us whole. We severed rings do not have the power to reattach ourselves to the magnet. The magnet must reattach to us. When at last each atom and each grain have rotated to face the Suffering God, ring after ring in order, the severed parts of our own hearts reunite; and as Man is reunited with himself, so he is reunited with his other self, who is Woman. In no other way can lovers be penetrated with the power to love better than they have it in themselves to do.

The imperfection of mortal love has a cure because it is a disease. But the other problem with mortal love, which I call its insufficiency, cannot be cured, because it is not a disease. What I mean by its insufficiency is the fact that even when we do love well, mortal love is not enough. It was never intended to be enough. Not because of its imperfection, not because we love so poorly, but in itself and by its essence, it is not enough. For all its beauty, *just because* of its beauty, it cannot satisfy us completely, and the more deeply anyone loves, the more keenly he feels this to be true. The key that unlocks the riddle is that mortal love wants immortal love. The supernatural purpose of mortal love, and the cause of its sweet sorrow, is to awaken in us the longing for that greater love which alone can give us all that we long for. In a certain manner of speaking, not even the grace of God suffices for this longing. It wants God Himself, in person. We may not understand this desire. We may deny it. We may be unable to give a name to it. We may even give it the wrong name, confuse it with some other want. None of that stops us from wanting it.

Ultimately, all perishable beauty points beyond itself to the imperishable beauty. "Question the beautiful earth," writes St. Augustine. "Question the beautiful sea; question the beautiful air, diffused and spread abroad; question the beautiful heavens; question the arrangement of the constellations; question the sun brightening the day by its effulgence; question the moon, tempering by its splendor the darkness of the ensuing night; question the living creatures that move about in the water, those that remain on land, and those that flit through the air . . . question all these things and all will answer: 'Behold and see! We are beautiful.' Their beauty is their confession. Who made these beautiful transitory things unless it be the unchanging Beauty?"[5]

If the beauty of even inanimate creatures like the sun and moon, even irrational creatures like the air and constellations, even transitory creatures like the fish and birds, arouses the unappeasable longing for the imperishable Beauty of God, how much more so the beauty of love between living, rational, immortal men and women, who are jointly made in His image?

Although the other kinds of human love are not the subject of this book, what I have been saying about erotic love is true of each of them, too, each in its way. The love between husband and wife reflects something about God, but so does the love between parents and children, between brothers and sisters, between good masters and faithful servants, between friends, between partners in a cause. Every kind of created love reflects a different color of the Uncreated Love, as light is refracted through a prism. Each is the icon of some aspect of its Creator. Consider the love of a father for his child. Skeptics say that we project mortal fatherhood onto a cosmic screen and call it God the Father, but it is the other way around; God is the Father from whom earthly fathers take their name. That is why everything good in a child's earthly father makes it easier for him to love the Father, and why everything bad in him makes it harder.

Now obviously, if manifold kinds of human love are needed to refract the manifold yet single love of God, then erotic love cannot do all that work by itself. One color is not the whole spectrum. Even so, the union of husband and wife mirrors a certain aspect of divine love better than any other love can. It reflects the union that the Bridegroom intends with his people, the final consummation, the Marriage that leaves nothing to be desired.

Since God does not need us, why does He care for us, how could the Lover of Souls even bear such a name? The very idea of a God of love was a stumbling block for the ancient philosophers, for whom God was less a person than a theorem, "thought thinking itself." But suppose we begin at the other end; suppose it is actually true. What then? If God loves us even though He has no need of us, then the only remaining possibility is that love is not just something that He does, but what He is. "Impossible," one thinks. "Love is a relation among persons, but God is only one." But what if the One God is an eternal burning union of Three Persons? Is this so hard to believe? Don't the husband, the wife, and the living love between them provide a flashing finite glimpse of how Three might be infinitely One?

I said that the longing insufficiency of human love is incurable, because it is not a disease. But no human longing is made in vain. For thirst there is water; for hunger, food; for sorrow, solace; for wonder, knowledge; for weariness, rest. Water, food, solace, knowledge, rest, each of these is a created thing. Now what if there is some created longing that cannot be satisfied by anything in the created world? If our axiom is true, then this does not show that there is no satisfaction for this longing, but that its satisfaction lies beyond the created world. Now for the first part of the double longing of human spouses, fulfillment is in this world, for it lies in each other. But just because this love is so lovely, its longing lights another longing. As candle lights candle, their desire for each other kindles a desire for the Love of which their love is but a reflection. For that second part of their double longing, the fulfillment is neither in each other nor in any created thing. Does this make their union irrelevant? Say rather that it gives their union a new foundation and meaning, redirecting it outward and upward to the Creator.

For what would it profit them to give themselves to each other *instead* of to that Love? How could such refusal not utterly subvert them? Their love for each other can come into its own only if they are no longer their own. Their gift to each other must become a way in which they give themselves to the Giver. It is not enough to walk toward each other; together they must walk into Him. How could they stop now? How could they not go on?

Acknowledgments

On a dark night,
Kindled in love with yearnings—
O, happy chance!—
I went forth without being observed,
My house being now at rest.
        —John of the Cross, *Dark Night of the Soul*

As this book goes forth, I hope not without being observed, I am kindled with gratitude to those who have loved me: chiefly my parents, through whom I came to be; my wife, through whom I came to understand; my friends, with whom I found shared cause; and the author of all these happy chances, through whom I came to myself. May I be forgiven for anything I have written unworthily, and may it neither mislead nor scandalize. If anything I have written is true, may it give light to others.

Particular thanks to Mitchell Muncy and Tom Spence, who talked me into the disturbance of writing the book in the first place. My house is now at rest.

Notes

Chapter 1: Does Sex Have to Mean Something?

1. Aldous Huxley, *Brave New World*, chapter 6.
2. The earlier version of the chapter appeared in *Touchstone*, June–July 2005.

Chapter 2: The Meaning of the Sexual Powers

1. Naomi Wolf, *Promiscuities: The Secret Struggle for Womanhood* (New York: Random House, 1997), quoted in Wendy Shalit, "Daughters of the (Sexual) Revolution," *Commentary*, December 1997, 42–45.
2. Katie Roiphe, *Last Night in Paradise: Sex and Morals at the Century's End* (New York: Little, Brown, and Company, 1997), quoted in Maggie Gallagher, "Second Thoughts," *National Review*, March 24, 1997, 51–52, at 52.
3. Gregory A. Freeman, "Bug Chasers: The Men Who Long to Be HIV+," *Rolling Stone*, February 6, 2003, 915. Freeman's article has been widely criticized in the homosexual media for reporting an alleged statement by Bob Cabaj, director of behavioral health services for San Francisco County and past president of both the Gay and Lesbian Medical Association and the Association of Gay and Lesbian Psychiatrists, that 25 percent of newly infected homosexual men fall into a category of bug chasers (a statement

which Cabaj now denies making). But although activists and public-health professionals debate how prevalent the phenomenon may be, few deny its reality. For discussion, see Seth Mnookin, "Is *Rolling Stone*'s HIV Story Wildly Exaggerated?" *Newsweek* Web exclusive, January 23, 2003; Andrew Sullivan, "Sex- and Death-Crazed Gays Play Viral Russian Roulette!" Salon.com, January 24, 2004; Phillip Matier and Andrew Rose, "Uproar Over S.F. Health Official's Rolling Stone AIDS quote," *San Francisco Chronicle* (January 27, 2003); Tammy Bruce, "Bug Chasers and the Thought Police," FrontPage Magazine, January 29, 2003; and Mubarak Dahir, "Could 'bug chasing' be more serious than we want to admit?" *Bay Windows* online, January 30, 2003.

4. Norval Glenn and Elizabeth Marquardt, "Hooking Up, Hanging Out, and Hoping for Mr. Right: College Women on Dating and Mating Today," a report by the Institute for American Values to the Independent Women's Forum (2001).

5. Benoit Denizet-Lewis, "Friends, Friends With Benefits, and the Benefits of the Local Mall," *New York Times Magazine*, May 30, 2004. The author writes, "underneath the teenage bravado I heard so often are mixed feelings about an activity that can leave them feeling depressed, confused and guilty."

6. I adapt these two conditions from Robert C. Koons, *Realism Regained: An Exact Theory of Causation, Teleology, and the Mind* (Oxford: Oxford University Press, 2000). The change lies in the second of the two conditions: Rather than requiring that the fact that P brings about Q be part of the efficient cause of P, I say that it must be part of the explanation of P, leaving open the possibility that final cause is a fundamental and irreducible category of explanation, a possibility which Koons also now accepts (personal communication).

7. See Nicholas Eberstadt, "World Population Implosion? Speculations About the Demographics of De-population," *The Public Interest*, Fall 1997; *What if It's a World Population Implosion? Speculations about Global De-population*, Harvard Center for Population and Development Studies (March 1998); and "The Population Implosion," *Foreign Policy*, March 2001.

8. Sara McLanahan and Gary Sandefur, *Growing Up with a Single Parent: What Hurts, What Helps* (Cambridge, MA: Harvard University Press, 1994), 38.

9. René König, "Sociological Introduction [to the family]," *International Encyclopedia of Comparative Law* 4, no. 1 (1974): 42–43.

10. I expand on this crucial point in chapter 4. Not all forms of total self-gift require exclusivity; the uniqueness of sexual self-giving requires explanation, which I provide at that time.

11. The rest of this paragraph is closely indebted to John Finnis. See, for example, Finnis, "The Good of Marriage and the Morality of Sexual Relations: Some Philosophical and Historical Observations," *American Journal of Jurisprudence* 42 (1997), 97–134.

Chapter 3: The Meaning of Sexual Differences

1. Larry Cahill, "Why Sex Matters for Neuroscience," *Nature Reviews: Neuroscience* 7 (2006), 477–84. See also Larry Cahill, "His Brain, Her Brain," *Scientific American* 292, no. 5 (2005): 40–47.

2. Doreen Kimura, "Sex Differences in the Brain," *Scientific American* 267, no. 3 (1992): 119–25.

3. Cahill, "Why Sex Matters for Neuroscience."

4. The statement that "The brain secretes thought as the liver secretes bile," often attributed incorrectly to the eighteenth-century physician and lawyer Pierre Cabanis, is apparently due to the nineteenth-century physiologist Jacob Moleschott.

5. I borrow this crisp formulation from Robert P. George, *The Clash of Orthodoxies* (Wilmington, DE: ISI Books, 2001), 42, who in turn borrows it from Luke Gormally, *Euthanasia, Clinical Practice and the Law* (London: Lineacre Center, 1994), 111–66.

6. See, for example, Center for Applications of Psychological Types, "Estimated Frequencies of the Types in the United States Population," http://www.capt.org/mbti-assessment/estimated-frequencies.htm.

7. For example, see Robert R. McCrae and Oliver P. John, "An Introduction to the Five-Factor Model and its Applications," *Journal of Personality* 60, no. 2 (1992): 175–215. A "factor" is a statistical construct reflecting a pattern of covariation among a large number of other quantities.

8. See Alan Feingold, "Gender Differences in Personality: A Meta-Analysis," *Psychological Bulletin* 116, no. 3 (1994): 429–56; Paul T. Costa Jr., Antonio Terracciano, and Robert R. McCrae, "Gender Differences in Personality Traits Across Cultures: Robust and Surprising Findings," *Journal of Personality and Social Psychology* 81, no. 2 (2001): 322–31. Costa, et al., perform new research which broadens Feingold's conclusions about sex differences to a wider range of cultures and personality traits.

9. Costa, Terracciano, and McCrae, 329.

10. Am I exaggerating? Isn't this view outré? On the contrary, quite a few philosophers and legal scholars, perhaps the majority, now take it as axiomatic. They may distinguish among animals with different functional capacities—just as they distinguish among humans with different functional capacities—awarding "personhood" to some and denying it to others. However, they consider the distinction between humans and non-humans per se as arbitrary, prejudicial, and invidious. As I discover in my own teaching, they pass on this view to their students, most of whom swallow it whole.

11. I borrow the grammatical analogy from Darrell Dobbs, "Family Matters: Aristotle's Appreciation of Women and the Plural Structure of Society," *American Political Science Review* 90, no. 1 (1996): 74–89. He is not responsible for the use I make of it.

12. Interview with Alice von Hildebrand, Zenit news service, November 23, 2003, http://www.zenit.org/article-8793?1=english.

13. Edith Stein, *Essays on Woman,* 2nd ed., trans. Freda Mary Oben, comprising Volume 2 of Lucy Gelber and Romaeus Leuven, *Collected Works of Edith Stein* (Washington, DC: ICS Publications, 1996).

14. The verb is applied to the husband in 1 Timothy 3:4, 5, 12; the noun is applied to the wife in 1 Timothy 5:14. Literally, *oikodespotes* means "house despot," which is even stronger than the rendering I have offered, "ruler of the house." Other glimpses of St. Paul's view of the thoroughly mutual subordination of man and woman, husband and wife—equal in dignity, yet with different places in the dance—are found in 1 Corinthians 11:11–12 and Ephesians 5:21–32.

15. See, for example, David Popenoe, *Life Without Father* (Cambridge, MA: Harvard, 1996).

Chapter 4: The Meaning of Sexual Love

1. Sam Cooke, *Wonderful World*, from the album *The Wonderful World of Sam Cooke* (Keen Records, 1960).

2. "It is in the nature of love to bind itself, and the institution of marriage merely paid the average man the compliment of taking him at his word." G. K. Chesterton, "A Defense of Rash Vows," in *The Defendant* (New York: Dodd Mead, and Co., 1902), 23.

3. Josef Pieper, trans. Richard and Clara Winston, *About Love* (Chicago: Franciscan Herald Press, 1974), quoted in *Josef Pieper: An Anthology* (San Francisco: Ignatius Press, 1989), 28–29, emphasis added.

4. Corinthians 13:8—often quoted, often doubted, but the psychology and ontology are precisely accurate.

5. Song of Songs 6:3a (this and all subsequent quotations RSV).

6. I am quoting from the *Summa* of the great medieval thinker Thomas Aquinas, I, Q. 29, Art. 3.

7. Mystical writers do speak of stages of perfection, which they call purgative, illuminative, and unitive. However, they are speaking not of erotic love but of that love which erotic love imperfectly and confusedly reflects.

8. Song of Songs 1:7, 2:16, 6:2–3. The Shulammite is also courted by the king. According to the more traditional reading, the king and the one who pastures his flock among the lilies are the same person. Allegorically, the Shulammite is often then viewed as representing the soul, who is courted by God. I follow an alternative reading which distinguishes the king from the one who pastures his flock among the lilies and makes them competitors; the Shulammite intrepidly spurns the king's covetous advances in favor of her shepherd lover. In this case, the allegory makes the king in all his pomp represent the earthly alternative to the love of God, an alternative that the soul successfully resists. The difference in interpretation makes no essential difference to the argument I advance in this chapter.

9. Dante Alighieri, *La Vita Nuova,* trans. Barbara Reynolds (New York: Penguin, 1969), section 1, 29. I have inserted the literal sense of the Latin.

10. John 3:3–12.

11. *La Vita Nuova,* 29–30. Here and twice later, I have reinserted the translator's English renderings of the Latin sentences, which she puts in the notes.

12. *La Vita Nuova,* 30.

13. "The spirit of the senses" may also be translated "the animate [or animal] principle."

14. The translator renders this word as "source of joy."

15. See Charles Williams, *The Figure of Beatrice: A Study in Dante* (London: Faber and Faber, 1943).

16. The makers of cosmetics try hard to simulate this luminosity, but it has nothing to do with the shininess of skin.

17. In a parody of the vision, the eyes may also be affected in the furthest extremity of lust; but in a different way. Rather than a luster that she radiates, the light seems more like the burning of fire. There is no feeling that the beloved is too wonderful to look at, but only a craving to look.

18. *La Vita Nuova,* 30.

19. Song of Songs 8:12.

20. Ibid, 4:12. The expression "sister" is not to be taken literally but as an expression of intimacy.
21. Ibid., 8:6.
22. Ibid., 1:5–6.
23. Ibid., 1:2.
24. Ibid., 5:6–9.
25. John of the Cross, *Spiritual Canticle,* 9.
26. I may add that although romantic love is one of the strongest and most common conduits for this second longing, it can be awakened by many other experiences as well, even by such small things as "the smell of a bonfire, the sound of wild ducks flying overhead, the title of *The Well at the World's End,* the opening lines of *Kubla Khan,* the morning cobwebs in late summer, or the noise of falling waves." The quotation is from C. S. Lewis, whose discussion of this longing is unusually illuminating. See *The Pilgrim's Regress,* preface to 3rd ed. (New York: Bantam Books, 1986, orig. 1943), xii.
27. Song of Songs 3:5.
28. Ibid., 2:5–6.

Chapter 5: The Meaning of Sexual Beauty

1. The other kind is an active potentiality, a potentiality for *bringing about* change.
2. Some readers will be tempted to add, "if they haven't gone to sleep." Lacking the sense of ritual, some men do doze off. We take this eccentricity of our own time so much for granted that we project it onto all times, but taking it in the long view, it is an aberration and mutilation. As plant nature expresses itself automatically by exuding saps and resins, and beast nature expresses itself instinctually by emitting hoots and cries, so human nature expresses itself rationally by devising rituals and music.

Chapter 6: The Meaning of Sexual Purity

1. In the sense of "full of vitality and spirit."
2. John Bunyan, *The Pilgrim's Progress from This World to That Which Is to Come, and Grace Abounding to the Chief of Sinners,* preface by W. Clark Gilpin (New York: Random House, 2004), 235.
3. Aristotle, *Nicomachean Ethics,* 2.6.1107a.

Chapter 7: Transcendence

1. Bernard of Clairvaux, *Song of Songs I*, Sermon 7, in *The Works of Bernard of Clairvaux*, Vol. II, trans. Kilian Walsh, O.C.S.O. (Kalamazoo, MI: Cistercian Publications, 1981), 38–39.

2. Thomas Aquinas, *Summa Theologica*, I–II, Q. 2, Art. 8.

3. The remark is made by a soul in heaven to an inhabitant of hell who has been offered the chance to leave, in the novella of C. S. Lewis, *The Great Divorce: A Dream* (New York: HarperCollins, 2001, orig. 1946), 99.

4. I borrow this image from Peter Kreeft, who has used it in at least three of his wonderful books, including *Love Is Stronger Than Death* (San Francisco: Ignatius Press, 1999, orig. 1979), 14–15.

5. Augustine of Hippo, Sermon 241.2, from *Writings of Saint Augustine*, Volume 38, trans. Mary Sarah Muldowney, R.S.M. (New York: Fathers of the Church, Inc., 1947), 256. I have replaced the word "acknowledgment" with the word "confession," more accurately reflecting the Latin original, *confessio*.

Index